Rona Orme is the Children's Missioner for the Diocese of Peterborough. She lived in a small Devon village for 25 years before moving to Northampton in 2007. Passionate about working with children and families, Rona was responsible for establishing a new congregation for families with children under the age of eight in her Devon village, which continues to thrive. She is the author of *Rural Children, Rural Church* (Church House Publishing, 2007), which explores mission opportunities in the countryside, *Creative Mission* (Barnabas for Children, 2011) and *More Creative Mission* (Barnabas for Children, 2013). She is now involved with leading WoW (Worship on Wednesdays) for children and adults together in a primary school. Rona is a Reader in the Church of England.

Published by
The Bible Reading Fellowship
15 The Chambers, Vineyard
Abingdon OX14 3FE
United Kingdom
Tel: +44 (0)1865 319700
Email: enquiries@brf.org.uk
Website: www.brf.org.uk
BRF is a Registered Charity

ISBN 978 1 84101 662 7

First published 2015
10 9 8 7 6 5 4 3 2 1 0
All rights reserved

Acknowledgements

Unless otherwise stated, scripture quotations are taken from the Contemporary English Version of the Bible published by HarperCollins Publishers, copyright © 1991, 1992, 1995 American Bible Society.

Scripture quotations taken from The Holy Bible, New International Version (Anglicised edition) copyright © 1979, 1984, 2011 by Biblica. Used by permission of Hodder & Stoughton Publishers, an Hachette UK company. All rights reserved. 'NIV' is a registered trademark of Biblica. UK trademark number 1448790.

Scripture quotations from the Good News Bible published by The Bible Societies/ HarperCollins Publishers Ltd, UK © American Bible Society 1966, 1971, 1976, 1992, used with permission.

Extracts from the Authorised Version of the Bible (The King James Bible), the rights in which are vested in the Crown, are reproduced by permission of the Crown's Patentee, Cambridge University Press.

Cover photos (left to right): © Tuna Sarikaya/Hemera/Thinkstock; © Paha_L/iStock/ Thinkstock (also woman in middle); © syntika/iStock/Thinkstock (also pink little girl silhouette); © Sylwia Nowik/Hemera/Thinkstock (boy and girl); © Pavel Losevsky/Hemera/ Thinkstock (orange and purple silhouettes)

Every effort has been made to trace and contact copyright owners for material used in this resource. We apologise for any inadvertent omissions or errors, and would ask those concerned to contact us so that full acknowledgement can be made in the future.

A catalogue record for this book is available from the British Library

Printed and bound by CPI Group (UK) Ltd, Croydon CR0 4YY

50 Praise, Pray and Play Sessions

Easy-to-run all-age outlines for use throughout the week

Rona Orme

Acknowledgements

I love leading WoW (Worship on Wednesday). I love discussing theology with children; I love the privilege of being able to pray with families; I love the opportunity to play as we reflect on the things of God. Thank you to all the children and adults who have taught me how to lead and enjoy WoW. I am grateful to the Revd Jenny Parkin, our former parish priest, who helped set up WoW and gave me so much encouragement. Particular thanks must go to Mrs Lorraine Schofield, head teacher of Wootton Primary School, where we meet, and her staff for allowing us to use the studio and offering us such a warm welcome. I also acknowledge the prayerful support of the Revd Miles Baker, the Revd Lakshmi Jeffreys, Paula Lawrence, Evie McNally, Dawn Stokes, Chris Burnett and my colleagues in leading WoW week by week.

This book would not have been written without the blessing of sabbatical leave granted by the Diocese of Peterborough and the careful editorial work of Olivia Warburton and Lisa Cherrett at BRF.

When I was at school, I learned the following prayer by St Ignatius Loyola: 'Teach us, good Lord, to serve thee as thou deservest; to give and not to count the cost, to fight and not to heed the wounds, to toil and not to seek for rest, to labour and not to ask for any reward save the joy of knowing that we do thy will.'

I did not realise all those years ago that this was a prayer about discipleship. It has been my constant companion through times of joy and despondency. I pray that those I lead in WoW, and those of you reading this book, will grow more like Christ as you try to follow him. As Dietrich Bonhoeffer wrote, 'Christianity without discipleship is always Christianity without Christ' (*The Cost of Discipleship*, 1937).

Contents

*

Introduction

Jesus told his disciples:
Go to the people of all nations and make them my disciples.
Baptise them in the name of the Father, the Son, and the
Holy Spirit, and teach them to do everything I have told
you. I will be with you always, even until the end of the
world.

MATTHEW 28:19–20

I have taken this instruction seriously for many years and have
tried to follow it. Across the decades, my response has taken many
forms, and the material in this book comes from my latest attempt.
The gathering I lead is called WoW (Worship on Wednesday) and
we meet in the dance studio of a school by permission of the head
teacher. We offer simple refreshments (tea or coffee, using hot water
from a flask, squash, biscuits and sometimes fruit) as the school
day ends. The refreshments are set out on a table in the corridor (as
food is not permitted in the studio) where all the rapidly departing
pupils walk by. We have gathered in some children and families
simply because they have noticed the biscuits and asked what we
were doing.

We gather, children and adults together, in a range of different
family formats. We do not use consent forms, so children are
required to bring an adult with them to share the session. Parents
and grandparents take part, and sometimes they take responsibility
for children who are not their own. For me, it is important to lead
children into faith and along the path of discipleship in the context
of their families. It is so hard for children who come to faith on
their own without the support and involvement of their families.
I hope to create a space where children and their families can
explore faith together, either extending their existing understanding
of God's love for them and what that might mean or introducing

them together to the possibilities of trying to follow Jesus as their Saviour.

That is not to say the group never splits according to age. In our group, children love the messier and more active pursuits, while most of the adults move away from them. However, we love praying together and for each other; sharing Bible stories and laughing.

Some children and adults love colouring, and others prefer chat or fingering sand or folding paper. Visitors to WoW comment that most of the response activities are done by a mix of children and adults all helping each other to share resources, ideas or ways to finish. I also relish creating a space where children and adults can teach each other and share their insights and prayers. Our numbers have varied over the years from just a dozen to over 30. It has taken a long time to build friendships.

Once we move into the studio (taking off our shoes—to protect the floor, though the action has a holy resonance, too), we share fun, Bible study, response time, prayer and conversation. We certainly cover worship, fellowship, discipleship and ministry to each other and we often manage to include mission (Rick Warren's five key activities for any church).[1] Children, as well as adults, deserve the chance to enjoy the full experience of being a Christian. For some of the group, WoW is the only church they know. For others, WoW is a midweek congregation of the parish church that they may attend weekly or occasionally. A third group are active members of other churches and denominations who delight in the 'all together' nature of WoW.

The original design brief for WoW included these aims.

- **Forty minutes maximum**, so that it would be possible to plan a detailed timetable of activities and not deter people by taking up too much time.
- **Focus on primary-aged children**, while including pointers and challenge for adults. Adults new to exploring faith may be just as spiritually young as those who are, chronologically,

decades younger. Younger family members are also welcome and often take a full part.

- **Mix of styles, activities and ways of doing things across several sessions**, the principle being that if someone does not like the quiet contemplation in one week, they know it will be livelier or different the next time.
- **Clear aim for each session**, so that the leaders know what their focus is, making it easier to plan, and so that those taking part understand the purpose of that week.
- **Boy-friendly**—an important aim when the leadership has been female. As author Nick Harding explains, boys often need a different approach.[2]
- **Strong on relationship-building**. The small group size allows people to get to know each other, although activities often need to be planned to ensure that new people feel welcome.
- **Encouraging response, discipleship and all-age activity**. This is the area that fascinates and challenges me: read on for more detail.
- **Informal and fun**.
- **Fairtrade refreshments and resources where possible**. Fairtrade is important in itself, but WoW can be a vehicle for publicising it.

These aims developed over several months as the vision for WoW was cast in the midst of much prayer, reading and discussion. I was working through a *Mission-Shaped Ministry* course,[3] so there was an opportunity to develop the model for WoW as part of my studies. This amount of thinking and praying was much needed.

I was also well aware that some of the ways we have worked with children in the past have not helped them grow as disciples. The Revd Dr Sandra Millar, Church of England Head of Projects and Developments, has pointed out that children are 'co-disciples'. Interviewed in the *Church Times*, she notes that the earlier, very educational, model of working with children, and the more recent idea that we need to entertain them, have not proved to be particularly effective.[4] The challenge for me was to find a way that had a much stronger focus on discipleship while still planning for fun and learning from the Bible. I am not alone in thinking this way. Paul Moore, one of the developers of Messy Church, writes, 'From the moment they walk in the door [of Messy Church at St Wilfrid's, Cowplain], everything we do is about making disciples.'[5] I cannot recommend his book too warmly.

Living a Christian life is often described as a journey or pilgrimage. In *Working from a Place of Rest*, Tony Horsfall suggests that there are three aspects to this journey.[6]

- The 'discipleship journey of obedience and faith' particularly affects the outward aspect of life, such as decisions about where to live, what form of employment (paid or unpaid) to pursue and how to use our time as we try to live as disciples of Jesus. For children, this may include how often to pray, which books to read or videos to watch and how much help to give at home.
- The 'transformational journey' is about our more inward life, in which we develop our character and behaviour to become more like Jesus, and it particularly concerns how we respond to the challenges of life. Children experience this journey as they learn how to behave well in the playground, to welcome new children in class or to make sense of a long stay in hospital.
- The 'journey through life' is the chronological progression from birth to death.

These three journeys are intertwined.

Horsfall says that 'Christian discipleship can never be a part-time, half-hearted affair. It demands the offering of our lives to God... Spiritual formation takes time and a certain amount of discipline on our part as we cooperate with the work of the Spirit within us'.[7] He then suggests that there are three stages of maturing spiritually.

First we come to know that 'we are God's beloved children, loved by him unconditionally and eternally'. Then we become aware that 'Christ is now living his life within us', which means 'learning to live in dependency upon him'. Finally, 'as the outer shell of self-centredness and self-will is broken within us, so the life of Christ is released through us in an overflow of compassion and love to others'.

Horsfall mentions research suggesting that although the church plays a significant part in the early stages of spiritual development, ongoing spiritual formation happens as people develop their own spiritual practices to sustain themselves.[8] For those of us who work with children and families, this means that we must work hard to introduce them to a range of effective and attractive spiritual practices so that they can continue to grow in faith and discipleship on their own. The spiritual disciplines that Horsfall highlights are stillness, silence and solitude (to bring us closer to God), reflection, Bible meditation and contemplation (to receive God's truth and to reflect on what he may be doing in our lives), and worship, one of the main ways 'by which we are able to drink the living water'.[9] This means we must plan to include a range of activities that will teach and promote these disciplines across a range of weeks.

People come to faith gradually, usually through a series of events, experiences and discussions with Christians. I am well aware that, at WoW, we are all at different stages of faith development. Some families come along because they seek friendship or something to do together as a family after school. We aim to provide them with Christian fellowship and fun. Others arrive because they want their children to know some of the stories of the Bible. That is one of the easier needs to meet. A third group want to know more about Jesus but are reluctant to come to a church service where they may be expected to know everything or to sit still and quietly. WoW is their church, so it is important to support these people, young and old, as they grow in faith and learn about discipleship. Yet others come because they have an active faith and want to learn more. They want to spend time with their own and other families in a Christian context. They sometimes have good knowledge of the Bible and what it means to be a follower of Jesus.

It would be impossible to plan specifically for the needs of each of these groups for every session, but it is important to bear their needs in mind over the course of a few weeks. Of course, the Holy Spirit often takes our simple planning and ensures that conversations and prayer activities are, in effect, tailored to each individual. Parents sometimes mention how a particular session has changed life a little in their home, and that is of enormous encouragement to us.

Each session of WoW ends with a challenge to take out into the world something of what we have learned or experienced. As the old 'Chorister's Prayer' says, 'What we have sung [or said] with our lips, may we believe in our hearts, and what we believe in our hearts may we show forth in our lives.'[10]

In *Making Disciples in Messy Church*, Paul Moore uses a circle of blessing[11] (see diagram below) to show how lives can be changed and how people of all ages can grow as disciples of Jesus.

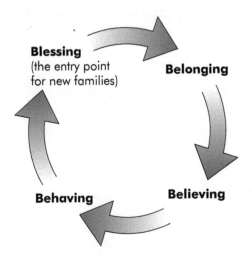

At WoW, our aim is to bless those who come along. If they feel blessed, then they may well want to belong, and we pray that, through belonging, they will come to believe. Belief in our creator, redeemer and sustainer will gradually change the way they behave—and then they too will bless others.

Notes

1   Rick Warren, in *The Purpose Driven Church* (Zondervan, 1995), identified five key purposes or activities for any church: worship, fellowship, discipleship, ministry and mission (pp. 95–109).
2   Nick Harding, *Boys, God and the Church* (Grove, 2007).
3   www.missionshapedministry.org.
4   Revd Dr Sandra Miller, Church of England Head of Projects and Developments, interviewed in *Church Times* (5 April 2013).
5   Paul Moore, *Making Disciples in Messy Church* (Messy Church, 2013), p. 64.
6   Tony Horsfall, *Working from a Place of Rest* (BRF, 2010), p. 21.
7   Horsfall, *Working from a Place of Rest*, p. 24.
8   Horsfall, *Working from a Place of Rest*, p. 91.
9   Horsfall, *Working from a Place of Rest*, pp. 93–94.
10 The Choristers' Prayer: www.rscm.com/info_resources/choristers_prayer.php.
11 Moore, *Making Disciples in Messy Church*, p. 18.

*

Getting started

Pray! Paul urges us in Romans 12:12 to 'never stop praying', so this is always the best way to start.

If you are hoping to start a new congregation or gathering, identify those who will pray with you and for you. Then start investigating a venue (your church may not be the right or most obvious answer) and discovering the right day and time slot. The material in this book was developed for a midweek session running at the end of the school day, but it would work equally well on a Saturday morning or later on a Sunday afternoon. To be effective, the session needs to run frequently and regularly. When looking for the right time slot, consider if you will be clashing with judo classes or the meeting of a uniformed group. Even if you do not actually clash, is there time for families to fit in a meal before hurrying on to another activity? Find out by chatting to parents. All of this research will take a couple of months if done thoroughly.

Start planning how you will publicise your gathering. Posters may raise a little interest but are unlikely to bring anyone in. When we launched WoW, we were allowed to include a brief explanation in the school newsletter. Because of our existing links with the school, we were also permitted to lead a 'taster' assembly to tell the children what would be happening. Since then, we have produced an invitation postcard that is offered to every child in the school at the beginning of each term, by permission of the head teacher. The card includes the dates and times for the term, a summary of who is invited (primary-aged children and their younger siblings, accompanied by a parent or carer) and an outline of what we will be doing. Our current summary mentions Bible stories, games, fun, refreshments, friends, crafts and prayer. See page 235 for a template that you can adapt for your own use.

The most effective way of attracting families to come along is by personal invitation. Who, in your existing congregation, can you excite with the vision? Ideally they will be a family or two with primary-aged children. Encourage them to start chatting to other families at the school gate about what is planned and what it might be like.

On pages 22–30 you will find a couple of 'welcome' sessions to use when you launch your group or at the beginning of a new school year (if you stop for the summer). These sessions emphasise the learning of names and the importance of fostering a sense of belonging. Building a community of people takes time and effort. Even in a fairly small school or village, not everyone will know each other.

Preparation

If necessary, get to know your space. We took in flasks of hot water until we realised that the school would give us access to their water heater. Now we fill our flasks with their hot water. We thought about where to position the refreshment table and what to put on it.

Once the group is running, encourage those coming along to bring biscuits or squash, as this helps them to feel involved. Parents have taken over the provision of refreshments at WoW so that the leaders do not have to bring them. Pay attention to any dietary restrictions. Some children are not able to eat chocolate, so substitute something else, preferably for the whole group. Check with parents about the need to substitute other foods for those who cannot eat gluten or who have diabetes. Dietary restrictions affect the general refreshments served as well as some of the suggestions within the sessions.

The studio where WoW takes place has enough space for us to set out the room beforehand with areas for different sections— gathering and games involving movement; welcome and sharing the Bible story, joint prayer and challenge; and response activities. We use colourful plastic cloths on which to arrange the different response activities. We pack wipes, a rubbish sack and a towel each time, in case we need them. Identify where to find lavatories and dustpan and brush if necessary. You may need to take a first aid kit.

Sometimes the list of resources needed for a session may look long, but most of the items will be small. For WoW I usually carry everything needed for a session (excluding refreshments) in a backpack and two large shopping bags. The only exceptions are for the 'large-scale' activities involving big cardboard boxes. Either gather a collection of boxes that nest inside each other, so that several can be carried by one person, or negotiate a place to store them. If all else fails, use smaller boxes but this will be less fun, especially for boys. See the Equipment section, page 250, for a helpful list.

*

How to run a session

The key elements of each session are Gathering, Welcome, Bible input, Response, Prayer and Challenge. The sessions are grouped into sections. Each section has an overarching Bible verse that links all the material. Some groups may choose to learn it as a memory verse, and ideas are given for doing this, but it is not essential. Most sections also have a 'theme song' that could be learned and sung at each session in the series. Again, this is optional.

Although each session follows the same format, check the material as the activities do not always follow exactly the same timings. Occasionally more time is needed for the reflection or prayer towards the end than for the Bible input or craft.

Gathering

Children can consume their snacks at an amazing speed. Make sure that the gathering activity is ready to start with the first arrivals: this prevents children from running around the space (an opportunity for falls and tears) with nothing to do. Most of the suggested gathering activities can incorporate later arrivals.

It is best if everyone sits in a circle so that they can see each other, even if this means using rugs or mats to sit on the floor. Using the floor allows children and adults to loll or sprawl or wriggle without making chair noise. Those who are infirm may require a chair. Position any such chairs at the opposite side of the circle to the leader. The studio where WoW takes place has crash mats, so we arrange them to form an oblong for our main input.

Welcome

Sometimes, in a series of sessions (such as those on the fruit of the Spirit), it can be helpful to use the Welcome time to review what happened the previous week. It can also be good to ask how people got on with last week's challenge. Bear in mind that some families may have been absent and may feel uncomfortable if they do not know the answer. It can be helpful for the leader to recap without asking, 'Who remembers what we did last week?'

Bible input

Leave plenty of space for everyone to respond to the material. Do not try to explain every Bible story and what to think about it. Spiritual development is encouraged best when we ask questions and allow the Holy Spirit to direct the thoughts and responses of each individual. Do not shy away from asking deep, 'pondering' questions that would challenge an adult: children often delight in attempting to answer them. Always leave a few moments of silence after sharing the Bible passage before asking the suggested questions, to allow the power of the story to sink in.

Some of the Bible passages are written as 'raps' or informal poetry, which need to be performed with lots of expression. Other passages may need to be read thoughtfully and quietly. Aim to find a different way of presenting each passage according to its subject. Occasionally, play figures are used to illustrate or 'act' the story: be sure to find neutral figures (see Equipment, page 250). One of my sessions was diverted when the boys wanted to know why I had chosen a particular Lego® character, when I had just grabbed the nearest figures to hand.

At each session, provide copies of the Bible, including children's versions, with the day's passage marked so that it can be easily found. Bible storybooks can also be found that retell the passage, so make them available during the response time as another option. Children and adults often enjoy rereading the passage in a different version. This underlines the fact that the material always comes from the Bible.

Adapt the material and ideas to include children and adults with additional needs. 'Through the Roof' (see Resources, page 253) provides helpful ideas and links. For example, you may need to provide extra explanation for someone with visual impairment, perhaps giving them the chance to feel props before you use them. It may be a good idea to provide a buddy, to help someone with additional needs to take part as fully as possible. Discuss with the person whether they would prefer the same buddy each time or not.

There are some links to video clips. These can be used as part of a session or you could share the link so that families can watch them afterwards. We have a WoW page on Facebook so that web links can be shared there if desired.

Response

When we move from sharing the Bible story to giving opportunities to respond to it actively, I always say, 'You have a choice!' It has become a ritual that the children help me to chant. Explain the activities carefully so that good choices can be made, and expect the children to wait until all the choices have been outlined. You may have to reassure them that there are sufficient resources for them all. It can be helpful to invite everyone aged six to be first to make their choice, or everyone wearing purple, or some different category each time to stop momentary chaos. Once choices have been made, everyone usually settles down quickly.

Put the instructions for each craft on to a sheet of paper and provide a sample if necessary. Decide where the leaders will be needed. If there is a game to be played, one leader will have to lead or supervise it—or you could brief a parent beforehand on how to lead the game.

Prayer

It is important that the prayer section is not downgraded or even omitted. I have observed far too many holiday clubs and sessions for children where prayer has become an optional, or even forgotten, part. Remember that Romans 12:12, 'Pray at all times', applies as much to the sessions as to the preparation.

It is a good idea to teach everyone to sign 'AMEN' in British Sign Language, as this helps even the youngest to join in the response. Do this by making each hand into a fist and gently tapping the fists together so that the thumbs are side by side (see Resources, page 253, for a web link to watch this in action). The group may like to develop their own special way of saying 'Amen'. For example, it could be the 'rising Amen' in which everyone starts saying 'Aaa' quietly, getting louder into the 'men'. Another way is to say 'A-A-A... MEN-MEN-MEN', or ask the group to come up with their own idea.

If the group is bigger than about 20 people, there may be times when the prayer activity will be more effective split into two smaller groups. This may speed the process up, but it will also pull away from the sense of unity, so dividing in this way could be an occasional solution. At WoW, we often pray for each member of the group by name in the context of that session.

Challenge

The 'challenges' are intended to help people put what they have learned into action. Try to encourage some discussion about how the challenge could be achieved each week. The group will often come up with helpful suggestions and even radical ideas.

Some of the challenges involve collecting money. The suggested 5p may seem appropriate for some groups, but in wealthier areas you could select a more suitable amount to suggest.

Welcome

••

Christianity is based on invitation and welcome. Jesus said, 'Come to me and I will give you rest' (Matthew 11:28). Welcoming children and adults to the group, so that they can hear the invitation and good news of Jesus, needs good preparation. Consider the following.

- **Access:** Is the venue well-signed and will the door be open? Arrange to have someone at the door if necessary to assist with buggies, wheelchairs or directions.
- **Attention:** Do the leaders and helpers greet those attending with a smile and good eye contact, or do they prefer to chat to other members of the team? Are children greeted, down at their eye level, with the same courtesy? Are the leaders and helpers genuinely interested in those who come along?
- **Comfort:** Are the lavatories clearly marked and are they clean and well equipped?
- **Refreshments:** Does the choice of refreshments include gluten-free, healthier or vegetarian options?

I would not teach a Bible memory verse or expect people to sing at the earliest sessions. Older children and adults need to feel comfortable in a setting before they can join in with enthusiasm.

*

Jesus welcomes everyone

This session encourages everyone to learn each other's names. Knowing names, and being known, helps everyone to feel that they belong. Christians believe that God knows individuals by name, so it is important to show the same level of care. This session would work well when starting a new group or returning at the beginning of the school year after a break.

Key Bible verse

Jesus said, 'When you welcome even a child because of me, you welcome me. And when you welcome me, you welcome the one who sent me.'

MARK 9:37

Bible links

- Isaiah 43:1 (God calls us by name)
- Luke 5:1–11 (Jesus calls the fishermen)

You will need
- Bouncy ball
- A3 poster with 'Everyone can be part of God's kingdom' written around the edge
- Selection of at least six teddies
- Wristbands made from 2-cm sections of kitchen towel tube, slit to fit around wrist
- Stickers with 'Jesus welcomes me' on them
- Lengths of wool, preferably in a range of colours
- Pens; hole punch; scissors
- Water pistols; towel
- Large ball of string

Session aim

To understand that everyone is welcome in the group and in God's kingdom.

Gathering activity

Gather everyone into a circle and give one person the ball. Whoever holds the ball asks someone else their name. They then call out that name as they bounce the ball to the person. Keep going round the circle so that everyone is named and has a turn at bouncing. Make sure to welcome in new players as they arrive.

Welcome

Invite everyone to sit round in a circle. Pass the ball around the group, with the leader being challenged to remember everyone's name as they receive it. Then get everyone to turn to the person sitting next to them to say, 'You are welcome!'

Bible passage

Jesus always shared a welcome with all the people he met. This is how Jesus welcomed his first friends as he was walking by a lake.

Jesus was standing down by the lake.
People came to see him, they needed a break.
Jesus saw two boats pulled up on the shore.
He told the men who owned them they could catch more.
Jesus hopped in a boat, taught the crowd for a bit,
Then told the fishermen to head for the deep
And let down their nets to get a big haul
Of so many fish, their nets would be full.

'What?' exclaimed Peter. 'We've been working all night.
There are no fish round here, not one nibble, not a bite.
But if you say so, we'll do it once more.'
And then they had trouble getting back to the shore,
For the nets were full and starting to rip.
This had been a most successful fishing trip.

'Get away from me,' Peter said to the Lord.
'I feel sinful when I have you on board.'
'Don't be afraid,' Jesus said to them then.
'Soon you will catch not fish but men.'
They pulled up their boats and left them right there
To follow Jesus everywhere.

Ask these questions.
- What was the most surprising thing that happened that day?
- How would you have felt if you had been fishing with Peter?

Response activities

- **Poster:** Add your own name to the A3 poster.
- **Retell:** Use teddies to act out the story.
- **Wristband:** Decorate the tubing with pens and add a 'Jesus welcomes me' sticker. Make two holes at each end of the band. Thread wool through the holes to draw the sides together and fasten with a bow.
- **Large-scale:** If there is outdoor access, use water pistols to write 'Welcome' on the ground at the entrance. Make sure children are accompanied.

Back together

Ask everyone to line up alphabetically according to their first name. This is another chance to meet new people. Then return to the circle.

Prayer activity

Lay the A3 poster in the centre of the circle. Holding on to one end of the string, the leader tosses the ball across the circle to someone and says, 'Creator God, please bless [name].' The new person then takes hold of the string and throws the ball on to someone else as the leader says again, 'Creator God, please bless [name].' This continues until everyone has been prayed for by name and the ball of string has crisscrossed the centre to create a tangled web of links. At the end, ask everyone to lift the web of string up into the air and say 'Amen' together.

Tip: It is important that the leader leads the prayers at the early sessions until people gain confidence to speak out. It may be possible to encourage others to join the leader in repeating the prayer phrase.

Challenge

Invite a friend to come along to the next session.

God knows each of us by name

God loves and cares for each of us by name. Everyone needs to know how much they matter to God.

Key Bible verse

I have written your name on the palms of my hands.
ISAIAH 49:16B (GNB)

Bible links

- Genesis 21:1–7 (Isaac means 'laughter')
- Isaiah 45:3b (God calls people by name)
- Matthew 1:21 (Mary's son is to be called Jesus)
- John 1:40–42 (Jesus calls Simon 'Peter', the rock)

You will need
- Baby name books (borrowed from a library if necessary); A3 sheet of paper
- Bottles of ready-mixed paint with nozzle tops (or ready-mixed icing tubes)
- Paper plates (or plain biscuits)
- Wipes; towel
- A4 sheets showing the words 'The Lord says: "............ I can never forget you! I have written your name on the palms of my hands" (Isaiah 49:16).' (Artists may be able to draw a hand as the background to this photocopied sheet.)
- Bricks (wooden, Lego® or from another construction kit)
- Pens; paper

Session aim

To understand that God knows and loves everyone.

Gathering activity

Find out what different people's names mean, using the name books, and record the names on the A3 paper. Talk about why people were given their particular name: there may be some interesting stories.

Welcome

Invite everyone to line up according to their birthday date, from January to December. Then ask them to line up alphabetically according to their first name.

Bible passage

The Bible (open it and turn some pages) tells us that names matter. Just as parents today may give their children names that have a special meaning, there are lots of examples in the Bible of God's people doing that hundreds and thousands of years ago. Abraham and Sarah called their son Isaac, which means 'laughter', because God had given them joy and laughter in their old age. The name Jesus means 'the Lord saves'. Jesus himself looked at Simon, one of his first followers, and renamed him Peter, which means 'a rock'. Jesus saw that Simon Peter would be a strong part of the church in the years ahead. Then there was Saul, who changed his name to Paul after he became a Christian believer.

Names matter to us and they matter to God. There are two lovely sentences, near the middle of the Bible, where Isaiah says first that God has called each of us by name and then, even better, that he has our names written on the palms of his hands. This is like writing something on to our own hand as a reminder—except that our names never get washed off God's hands.

Ask these questions.

- How does it feel to know that God has your name written on the palm of his hand?
- Whose name would you write on your hand so that you never forget them?

Response activities

- **Name plate:** Use a bottle of paint to drizzle your own name on to a paper plate. (*Tip:* another, less messy, way of doing this would be to use tubes of ready-mixed icing to squeeze on to biscuits.)
- **Name sheet:** Add your own name in the space on an A4 sheet showing the words of Isaiah 49:16 (after the words 'The Lord says'), and then decorate the poster.
- **Build:** Use toy bricks to display your own name.
- **Game:** Play 'Human spelling' to create names (see Games on page 247). Younger children may need their initial written on to paper to help with the spelling. In a small group, written letters may be needed if there are not enough vowels to play with.

Back together

Reflect on how many millions of people's names God has written on the palms of his hands—now, back through history and into the future. God cares about all of them and each one of us.

Prayer activity

Ask if anyone wants to name someone who particularly needs prayer today. Explain that they do not have to give any details if they do not wish to. Then pray simply, 'Loving God, today we pray for [name all the people who have been mentioned] and for each of us here. Thank you that you know each of us by name. Amen'

Challenge

Explain that God likes us to keep on praying for the people who have been named. Ask for suggestions of ways to remember to keep on praying.

Creation and thanksgiving

This series can be followed at any time, but it fits particularly well in September and October as some of the sessions link with harvest. It is also possible to use individual sessions to fill a gap in the annual programme. A theme song for this series might be 'All good gifts around us' (the chorus of 'We plough the fields and scatter').

The Bible memory verse for this theme is 'The earth and everything on it belong to the Lord. The world and its people belong to him' (Psalm 24:1). To learn this verse, stretch both arms to 'draw' a large circle while saying, 'The earth and everything on it belong to the Lord'. Then hold arms out to the side and turn round in a complete circle for 'The world and its people belong to him'.

*

In the beginning

Whether the first chapter of Genesis is presented as giving a literal account of God creating the earth or as an early explanation of how things began, most children are fascinated by this story. Many children will have heard the Jewish and Christian creation story in RE, alongside other versions from different religions and traditions. This is an opportunity to set creation in the context of Christian worship and prayer.

Key Bible verse

In the beginning God created the heavens and the earth.
GENESIS 1:1

Bible links

* Genesis 1:1—2:4 (the story of creation)

You will need
* Inflatable globe
* World floor map; small stickers
* Marble run or other construction kit; marbles
* Pipe cleaners
* Dark-coloured paper; chalks
* Pictures of the elements of creation: dark, light, sky, tropical beach (showing land and sea), plants, sun, moon, stars, fish, birds, animals, people, earth (photographed from space); numerals 1–7

Session aim

To share God's delight in creating the world.

Gathering activity

Play 'catch' with an inflatable globe. Develop the activity by naming the person to whom the globe is about to be thrown, to help everyone to learn each other's names.

Welcome

Discuss all the places that members of the group have visited or where they have family or friends living. If a world floor mat is available, add small stickers to the places named. Otherwise, add the stickers to the inflatable globe.

Bible passage

Encourage everyone to join in the response **'And God was pleased with what he saw'** each time it is repeated.

In the beginning when God began to create,
The earth was a nothing and rather desolate.
There was a raging sea and it was totally dark.
God's Spirit was there but no park, no shark.
The first day, God said, 'Let there be light'
And he separated the day from the night:
And God was pleased with what he saw.

Next he divided the water into two
With sky between—this was day two:
And God was pleased with what he saw.

The third day he split the water from the land
And this was a mighty work of his hand.
The land he named 'earth' and the water 'sea'
And he stocked the ground with plants to seed:
And God was pleased with what he saw.

Then God put two great lights in the sky—
The moon to glow and the sun to see by—
And he added the stars to twinkle bright.
It was the fourth day when God made big light:
And God was pleased with what he saw.

Day five and God created the creatures
That swim in the sea, some with amazing features,
And others that fly in the sky above.
He made them with detail, with precision, with love:
And God was pleased with what he saw.

The sixth day God made the animals that live on the land
(Meerkats and zebras are all works of his hand),
And he made us in his image to rule on the earth
To look after the animals, to care for their worth:
And God was pleased with what he saw.

By the seventh day God had finished creation.
The beautiful earth was his revelation.
He'd made the whole universe, his task was complete
So he rested a day with the earth at his feet:*
And God was pleased with what he saw.

* Isaiah 66:1 refers to the Lord having the earth as his footstool.

Ask these questions.
- Why was God pleased with what he saw?
- What was the most important day of God's work?

Response activities

- **Design:** Make a marble run or something similar from a construction toy.
- **Invent:** Make animals from pipe cleaners.
- **Sketch:** Using dark paper and chalks, draw a scene from the creation story.
- **Order:** Use pictures of the different elements, and numerals, to tell the creation story.

Back together

Sing 'He's got the whole world in his hands', throwing an inflatable globe around the group during the chorus.

We include the names of people in the group in some verses— for example, 'He's got Jasmine, Bea and Judy in his hands'—and this is very popular.

Prayer activity

Using the world floor mat or inflatable globe, pray for the different people for whom stickers were placed during the Welcome activity, as well as for different areas of creation (mountains, sea, desert, rainforest and so on). Point at the different places as they are prayed for.

Challenge

Ask for suggestions for how to remember that God made the world, during the coming week.

The wonders of God's world

The popularity of nature programmes on television indicates how people are fascinated by the wonder and intricacy of the natural world. This is nothing new. The Psalms, written 3000 years ago, are full of amazement at the richness of God's world.

Key Bible verse

Don't you know? Haven't you heard? The Lord is the eternal God, Creator of the earth. He never gets weary or tired; his wisdom cannot be measured.

ISAIAH 40:28

Bible links

* Psalm 65 (praise and thanksgiving for God's action in his created world)

You will need
* Seven A2 sheets of paper, each headed with an extract from Psalm 65 (paraphrased) as follows:
  * Verse 1: Let us praise you, God.
  * Verse 2: All over the world people worship you.
  * Verse 9: You send rain to fill the streams so earth can produce its harvest.
  * Verse 10: You soak fields with rain so the young plants grow.
  * Verse 11: Your goodness provides a rich harvest.
  * Verse 12: The pastures are filled with sheep.
  * Verse 13: The valleys are full of corn: creation shouts for joy.

- Collage materials, such as seeds, wool, sheep's fleece, dried grass, cellophane, coloured tissue or crêpe paper, glitter, stickers and bubblewrap (think about the words of the psalm and the images that people may wish to illustrate)
- Pens; glue sticks; PVA gluepots and spreaders; sticky tape; scissors
- Construction toy such as Lego®

Session aim

To encourage delight and thanksgiving for God's creation.

Gathering activity

Play 'God created…'. Finish the phrase with something that God created. Everyone then has to make a shape in response. Children will have no difficulty in inventing shapes to represent 'light' or 'the sea'. Use all the different things included in last week's session: light, dark, sky, land, sea, plants, sun, moon, stars, fish, birds, animals, people and earth.

Welcome

Invite everyone to line up to create a rainbow with the clothes they are wearing. Start with red at one end and go through to violet at the other. It is extremely likely that there will be at least one person wearing red socks or pants that can peep through at a waistband, while several may be wearing a blue top. Some ingenuity and persuasion will be necessary to get people standing in the right place to show the whole spectrum.

Ask how people got on with the previous session's challenge of remembering that God made the world.

Bible passage

People have been praising and thanking God for the wonders of his creation for thousands of years. The following passage is a rewriting of a psalm, a poem-prayer, that David wrote more than 3000 years ago. Invite everyone to close their eyes as they listen, if they wish.

Praise, let us praise you, God!
Let us keep our promises to you
Because you answer our prayers.
From all over the world
People come to worship you...

You care for the land by sending us rain.
You fill the streams with water
So the earth can produce its harvest.
You soak the ploughed fields with rain
And soften the dry earth with showers.
Then can the young plants grow.
Your goodness provides a rich harvest.
With you, God, there is plenty.
The pastures are filled with sheep,
And joy fills the hillsides.
The fields are covered with flocks,
And the valleys are full of corn.
All of creation shouts for joy!
BASED ON PSALM 65:1–2, 9–13

Ask these questions.
• Which part of the poem-prayer made the best picture?
• What else could have been included in the poem-prayer?

Response activities

Using the headed A2 paper, create collages to illustrate the seven verses from Psalm 65. Work in small groups, each responsible for one or two of the collage sheets. This will help everyone to get to know each other better. Also provide a construction toy such as Lego® for those who prefer to be creative without using paper.

Back together

Sing 'He's got the whole world in his hands' in the same way as in the previous session.

Prayer activity

Invite everyone to move together around the artwork that has been produced. Pause at each collage sheet to give thanks to God, to pray for people who are hungry and for those who grow food, and to pray for those who care for our beautiful world. Include any construction models that have been made.

Challenge

Look out for signs of the rich harvest that God provides during the week ahead and remember to thank him.

Tip: This can be done in the supermarket as well as in the countryside.

Water—from sea to sip

Amazingly, 70 per cent of the earth's surface is covered by water and around 60 per cent of the human body consists of water. God has provided plenty of water but many of us use far more than our share. Washing machines use much water in action, but also require a lot of water for their manufacture. Many sources of clean drinking water have been contaminated by industrial processes or poor development. There are 125 million children under the age of five who do not have access to clean water and safe sanitation. This session thanks God for the provision of water and challenges everyone to think about how they use it.

Key Bible verse

Good news from far away refreshes like cold water when you are thirsty.
PROVERBS 25:25

Bible links

* Psalm 23:5 (God blesses us with an overflowing cup)
* Psalm 104:5–15 (the Creator gives water to bless humankind)

You will need
* Large sheet of paper with 'Water' written in the centre
* Brown cloth; inflatable globe; blue fabric; watering can with water; picture of oasis with animals drinking; model of bird or tree (don't worry about the scale); clump of grass; a vegetable; wine bottle; olive oil; pearl barley or similar
* Small plastic fizzy drink or water bottles with screw-top lids; ready-mixed blue paint; cheap cooking oil; funnel; sequins; parcel tape

- Water drop labyrinth (search online to source) (optional)
- Sheets of paper about 20 cm square
- Water pistols
- Jug of water; plastic tray
- Scissors

Session aim

To give thanks to God for the provision of water.

Gathering activity

On a large sheet of paper with 'Water' written in the middle, 'mind-map' all the different kinds of water and the places where it may be found (for example, sea, river, tap, car engine, fridge, drink and so on).

Welcome

Ask everyone to stand in a line across one side of the room. Then invite them to step forward as a response to each of the following statements:

- If you have drunk some plain water today, take one step forward.
- If you have had more than three drinks today, two steps forward.
- If you left the tap running while you cleaned your teeth, two steps forward.
- If you have watered a pot plant, one step forward.
- If you have watered plants in the garden, three steps forward.
- If you have had a shower in the last 24 hours, three steps forward.
- If you have had a bath in the last 24 hours, five steps forward.
- If you have been swimming in the past week, five steps forward.
- If you have had clean clothes every day this week, five steps forward.

Let the group think about how much water they have used recently. Then invite them to sit down to hear these amazing facts about water:

- 70 per cent of the earth's surface is covered by water (the leader may need to know that this represents 1,400,000,000 km^3, where 1 m^3 = 1000 litres).
- 69.5 per cent of total fresh water is locked away in the polar regions and Greenland.
- Less than 1 per cent of total water on earth is available for drinking and cooking.
- USA is the top consumer of water, at 575 litres per person a day.
- UK is 15th, at 150 litres per person each day.
- Ghana consumes 6 litres, Cambodia, Ethiopia, Haiti, Uganda each consume 5 litres on average, and Mozambique uses 4 litres.

Tip: Find the statistics for specific countries that members of the group may have come from or have links with.

Cleaning your teeth with the tap running uses nearly a whole litre of water.

How many times is water mentioned in the Bible? (A total of 636 times in the King James Bible and 387 in the Contemporary English Version.)

Bible passage

As one person reads this section of Psalm 104, another uses the objects to illustrate it.

A prayer-poem by King David

Spread a brown cloth out in the middle of the group.

You built foundations for the earth *(place globe on cloth)* and it will never be shaken.

You covered the earth with the ocean *(place blue fabric beside globe)* that rose above the mountains.

Then your voice thundered and the water flowed down the mountains *(sprinkle water from watering can on to the globe)* and through the valleys to the place you prepared.

Now you have set boundaries, so that the water will never flood the earth again. You provide streams of water in the hills and valleys, so that the donkeys and other wild animals can satisfy their thirst *(place picture of oasis on the cloth)*.

Birds build their nests nearby and sing in the trees *(place model bird or tree on the cloth)*.

From your home above, you send rain on the hills and water the earth *(create another sprinkle of water from the can)*.

You let the earth produce grass *(add grass to display)* for cattle, plants *(add vegetable)* for our food, wine *(add wine bottle)* to cheer us up, olive oil *(add bottle of oil)* for our skin, and grain *(sprinkle pearl barley)* for our health.

Ask these questions.
- Which part of the prayer-poem made you think about God?
- What would you add to the poem to praise God?

Response activities

- **Sea-in-a-bottle:** Put a squeeze of blue paint into a small plastic bottle. Use a funnel to add 2 cm of oil first; then fill two-thirds full with water. Drop in a few sequins to represent fish. Close the lid securely and seal with parcel tape. The bottle can then be shaken to watch a 'storm' settle.

- **Water drop labyrinth:** Slowly manipulate a bead of water round the labyrinth.
- **Cup:** Fold a square of paper to make a cup that will hold water (see Web references, page 242).
- **Water pistols:** Go outside and enjoy the water!

Back together

People in the UK use lots of water. Discuss ways to help people who live in areas of frequent drought. Lead the discussion towards raising money for a water charity (see Web references, page 242).

Prayer activity

Use one of the folded paper cups and a jug of water during the prayer time. Place a tray below to catch the overflow of water.

Creator God, thank you for the gift of water. *(Pour water into the cup, about one-quarter full.)*

Help us not to waste the water that we have. *(Pour more water until cup is half full.)*

We pray for everyone who will not have enough or clean water to drink today. *(Pour in more water, to three-quarters full.)*

And we pray for the organisations that help to provide good water for people in need. *(Pour water to the brim.)*

The Bible tells us that you want to bless us until the cup overflows. *(Pour in more water, to overflowing.)*

Thank you, generous God, in the name of Jesus. Amen

Challenge

Find out about charities that work to provide clean water for people in need and think about ways to raise some money for their work.

Note: Also ask if anyone has any food allergies, in preparation for the next session.

Food

This session introduces the idea of thanking God for food. Everyone has a favourite food and will be happy to talk about their preferences. Icing biscuits and prayers that involve eating will be popular.

Key Bible verse

God created these foods to be eaten with thankful hearts.
1 TIMOTHY 4:3

Bible links

* Luke 22:17–19 (Jesus thanks God for bread and wine)

You will need
* Bread roll in basket; wine glass
* Plain biscuits
* Sliced bread (*Tip:* to prevent the biscuit from cracking when spreading the icing, lay it on a slice of bread, which will act as a cushion)
* Icing (home-made water-icing, applied with plastic knives or spreaders, or ready-made icing from a tube)
* Edible sprinkles, such as hundreds and thousands, chocolate flakes and granulated sugar coloured with a few drops of food dye
* Paper plates
* Wipes and/or towel; antibacterial gel or wipes
* Cube 'nets' printed on thin card (see Templates, page 236)
* A2 paper; duct tape
* Pens; scissors; glue sticks; sticky tape
* A lemon with knife to cut it; jelly 'people' (additive-free or vegetarian ones can be found in some supermarkets); Smarties® or tiny pieces of chocolate; bread

Session aim

To thank God for food.

Gathering activity

Challenge everyone to pretend to be a range of foods. Examples could include pizza, jelly, sausages, cornflakes and banana.

Do not worry if, as leader, you have no idea how to make a shape for sausages: the children will be quick to produce ideas. Choose foods that are popular locally and have a recognisable shape.

Welcome

Invite everyone to 'line out' to vote for some of their favourite foods. For example, if they really like chips, they should stand at one end of the line (point to one side of the room), if they do not like them at all, they should stand at the opposite end, and if they like chips a bit, they should stand somewhere between the two ends. Again, use foods that will be known well by the group but make sure to include one or two that will cause a range of opinions, such as beetroot, rhubarb or cheese strings.

Sing 'All good gifts around us', the chorus of 'We plough the fields and scatter', learning it first if necessary.

Bible passage

Ask if anyone says Grace before a meal. What is a 'grace'? It is something that Jesus said and did. Listen to these words from the Bible.

Jesus took a cup of wine in his hands (*pick up the glass*) and gave thanks to God. Then he told the apostles, 'Take this wine and share it with each other. I tell you that I will not drink any more wine until God's kingdom comes.' Jesus took some bread in his hands (*pick up the bread roll*) and gave thanks for it. He broke the bread and handed it to his apostles (*pass the bread around, each person taking a little to taste*). Then he said, 'This is my body, which is given for you. Eat this as a way of remembering me!'

LUKE 22:17–19

Ask these questions.

- Why did Jesus always remember to thank God for food and drink?
- What did it feel like to share some of the bread?

Response activities

- **Biscuit:** Spread icing on to a plain biscuit and decorate with sprinkles. Think about all the lovely foods that God has given to his people.
- **Grace cube:** Add different praise and thank you words to each face of the cube 'net'. Explain that it can be used at meals to thank God for food. Cut out the shape, fold along the lines and then glue to make a cube. Sticky tape may be needed to keep it secure.
- **Large-scale:** Work together to spell out the words 'Thank you, God' on a sheet of A2 paper using pieces of duct tape.
- **Prepare:** Some older children may like to help prepare the items to be used in the prayer activity (see below) by cutting up the lemon or breaking the bread into small pieces. Ensure that hands are clean, by using antibacterial gel or wipes, before handling the food to be shared.

Back together

Ask for suggestions of favourite foods before singing 'All good gifts around us' once more.

Prayer activity

Explain that there are four tasting prayers with little things to eat, if people wish to try them, to guide them in how to pray.

- Lemon: to pray for things that are 'sharp' or sour in the world.
- Smarties: to thank God for something.
- Jelly 'people': to pray for someone who particularly needs prayer.
- Bread: to pray for what people need.

Challenge

If the group has been thinking about supporting a water-based charity, use this time to discuss the plan to fundraise. Otherwise, challenge everyone to give thanks to God for every meal they eat just as Jesus did. They can use the Grace cube if they have made one.

*

Nature provides

God provides food for all the plants and animals in the world—
and enough food for humans, if people remember to share the
resources of the earth. By pointing out how things work in nature,
Jesus taught that it is important to trust God to provide what is
required for each day.

Key Bible verse

'Your Father in heaven knows that you need all these.'
MATTHEW 6:32B

Bible links

* Matthew 6:25–34 (Do not worry, God will provide)

You will need
* Menu or takeaway flyer; picture or model of a bird; seed
  packet; sock; water bottle; crown; calendar
* Building noodles; small pots of water (or saucers); towel
* Paper; pens
* Paper shredder or pedal bin with lid
* Toy bricks (could be Jenga® style)

Session aim

To show that God provides for everyone.

Gathering activity

Play a version of Port and Starboard (see Games, page 248) with
Mountain, Sea, River, Pasture as the key words and Nature as the
central word.

Welcome

Recap the previous session on food. Remind the group of some of the favourite foods mentioned last time. Ask if anyone has remembered to say 'grace', a prayer of thanks, before or after a meal. Point out what lovely food God provides for us to eat.

Bible passage

Slowly set out the items that will be used to illustrate the story (see first bullet point under 'You will need'). Pause to allow everyone to be puzzled, then begin.

Jesus was sitting on a hillside, talking to the crowds of people who had come to listen to him. He said, 'Don't worry about what you are going to eat *(touch menu)* or what clothes you are going to wear *(touch sock)*. Life is about much more than fancy food and fabulous clothes. Look around you at the birds *(touch bird)*. They don't sow seeds *(touch seed packet)*. God provides for them all right. And I think you are worth much more than these lovely birds. Don't worry so much!

'Nor is it a good idea to fret about having the right clothes *(touch sock)*. God has provided gorgeous colours for the wild flowers that you can see, even though they will only last a day or two. I know that God will look after you even more closely. So don't worry about where your food *(touch menu)*, your drink *(touch water bottle)* or fine clothes *(touch sock)* will come from. God, your father in heaven, knows you need these things. It is better to think about living as God wishes and your place in the kingdom of heaven *(touch crown)*. You do not have to worry about tomorrow *(touch calendar)*, as God will provide what you need. Deal with today's problems today.'

Ask these questions.
- What might the crowds of people have talked about on their way home after listening to Jesus?
- Jesus talked about our place in heaven. What might that be like?

Response activities

- **Reminder:** Draw a sunflower with lots of petals.
- **Illustrations:** Make some of the things in today's story from building noodles, using water to stick the pieces together.
- **Worry bin:** Offer paper and pens for individuals to write things that worry them. Provide a small shredder (assess the risk for this) or pedal bin for the worries to be thrown away into God's care.
- **Large-scale:** Build a tower of worries from toy bricks and demolish it by pulling out bricks from the foundation layer.

Back together

Ask a few people to talk about what they have made.

Prayer activity

Use some of the things that have been made, or some of the story illustrations, to thank God for his provision. Sing 'All good gifts around us', the chorus of 'We plough the fields and scatter' (learning it first if necessary), after each item.

Challenge

Write or draw something to thank God for on each petal of the sunflower that people have drawn.

If the group is raising money for a charity project, suggest that they collect 5p for each thing they record on the sunflower.

Advent, Christmas and Epiphany

In Advent, the weeks leading up to Christmas, we have an opportunity to think about the preparations God made for Jesus to be born. The first two sessions focus on meetings, with both Zechariah and Mary listening to God's message as they meet Gabriel the angel. The third looks at our own meeting with God and how we hear his message. How did Zechariah and Mary respond? How do we respond to the good news of Christmas? Finally, the wise people meet Jesus after a dangerous encounter with Herod.

A theme song for these sessions could be a Christmas carol. 'O come, let us adore him', the chorus from 'O come, all ye faithful', would work well.

The Bible memory verse for this series is 'Don't be afraid!' (Luke 1:30). This could be learned by getting everyone to turn to others to say, 'Don't be afraid!'

Zechariah meets Gabriel

Zechariah, a priest in the temple, and his wife, Elizabeth, both led good lives in the view of God. They did not have any children and they were old. Although Zechariah was godly, he doubted the message that Gabriel the angel brought him. This led to his being struck dumb until after the promised baby was born.

Key Bible verse

'Don't be afraid!'

LUKE 1:30

Bible links

- Luke 1:5–23 (Zechariah is visited by an angel but doubts the message)
- Luke 1:57–79 (Zechariah names his son John and regains his speech to make an amazing prophecy)

You will need
- Incense stick and holder, plus matches (optional)
- Paper; pens; crayons; glue sticks; scissors
- Scraps of tissue and crêpe papers
- For memory game: tray; cloth to cover it; letters Z, A, J; incense stick; model angel; small box; wedding ring; small baby doll; picture of hands
- Scraperboard (see Equipment, page 251, for home-made version); scrapers
- Sheets of paper, each showing one name of Jesus: Jesus (the Lord is Salvation); Emmanuel (God with us); Prince of Peace; Saviour; Counsellor (someone who advises); Messiah (chosen one)

Session aim

To know that it is important to listen to God and accept what he says, however he speaks.

Gathering activity

The leader mimes various activities, which everyone has to copy. They then say what they think the activity was. Ideas for these mini-mimes include cleaning teeth; texting; opening a present; taking a dog for a walk; washing hands; opening a milk carton; making a hot drink; eating a bag of crisps; using a games console; skateboarding.

Welcome

Ask how easy it was to work out the mimed activities. Some will have been easier than others. In the Bible passage, someone called Zechariah doubted what he heard God saying to him. Zechariah ended up having to mime a lot of things for a very long time.

Zechariah was a priest in the temple and one of his jobs was to burn incense on the altar (*show incense stick, if using*). Incense plays a part in the account about Zechariah and the need to listen to God.

Bible passage

It was just an ordinary day—well, not exactly an ordinary day. An ordinary day would have meant that Zechariah would simply have gone to the temple in Jerusalem to take his part in the daily service of worship to God. He was a priest. He lived a good life and he tried to follow all God's commands and laws. He was married to Elizabeth. She was a good woman. They were sad because they had never had children.

While Zechariah was at the temple that day, his name was pulled out of the box for a very special task. That was when it stopped being an ordinary day and became an extraordinary one. Zechariah had been chosen to look after the burning of incense on the altar *(light incense stick, if using, and allow time for everyone to look at it)*.

Zechariah was concentrating on his job, so he did not notice the angel at first. I did say this was not an ordinary day! When Zechariah noticed the angel, he was startled—and afraid.

'Don't be afraid,' said the angel. 'God has heard your prayer, and so your dear wife, Elizabeth, is going to have a baby. You must make sure that the baby is called John. He will be an amazing person, like Elijah the prophet, and he will go ahead of the Lord to help people get ready for when the Lord comes.'

Zechariah shook his head in disbelief. 'How can this happen? Elizabeth and I are so old!'

'Silence!' said the angel. 'I am Gabriel, God's messenger, and you have doubted me. Now you will be unable to speak until my promise to you from God comes true.' Gabriel then left Zechariah stunned.

When Zechariah came out from the holy place, he could not speak to anyone. No words or sounds came out of his mouth. He went back home and soon Elizabeth did, indeed, find that she was expecting a baby. The months passed and still Zechariah could not speak. The baby, promised by Gabriel the angel, was born. All of the family wanted to call the baby Zechariah after his dad, but Elizabeth found herself saying that she wanted to call him John. The family thought this was a strange idea, for none of their relatives was called John.

Zechariah used his hands to call for something to write on. They watched as he wrote, 'His name is John.' At that moment Zechariah was able to speak again, and he and Elizabeth were filled with joy. There were such celebrations—but all the neighbours were filled with fear, as this was such a strange episode.

Ask these questions.
- Who was the most important person in this Bible passage?
- What was the most puzzling part of the story?
- How long did Zechariah have to keep quiet?

Introduce a minute of silence to remember something about the story. (Children will find this easier if they can watch the incense smoking.)

Response activities

- **Picture:** Draw or use collage to show something about Zechariah meeting Gabriel, God's angel and messenger.
- **Memory game:** See Games, page 248, for instructions.
- **Name sign:** Use a scraperboard to make a sign of your own name.
- **Mime:** Choose people to play the different parts (Zechariah, Gabriel, Elizabeth and other members of the family). Read the story again but with the characters miming what happens.

Back together

Names are really important. Everyone wanted to call Elizabeth's and Zechariah's baby son after his father. Only after he had written down the name 'John', which means 'God is gracious', was Zechariah able to speak again. Then Zechariah could not stop praising God.

The Bible gives a lot of names for Jesus. Place each name sheet down in turn and give its explanation.

- Jesus (the Lord is salvation)
- Emmanuel (God with us)
- Prince of Peace
- Saviour (one who saves)

- Counsellor (one who advises)
- Messiah (chosen one)

Prayer activity

Use the different 'names of Jesus' sheets to ask for prayer suggestions. For example, 'Prince of Peace' may prompt prayer for countries
facing war, and 'Counsellor' could suggest prayer for people who are
anxious.

Challenge

Zechariah doubted God and so he was unable to speak for a very
long time. This is a secret agent challenge to keep a short time of
silence each day to listen to God properly. Ask for ideas for making
this happen.

*

Mary meets Gabriel

Mary responded differently to Gabriel's message from God. Unlike Zechariah, she simply replied, 'I am the Lord's servant! Let it happen as you have said' (Luke 1:38). This session provides an opportunity to consider how we might respond to God.

Key Bible verse

'I am the Lord's servant! Let it happen as you have said.'
LUKE 1:38

Bible links

* Luke 1:26–38 (Gabriel, the angel, tells Mary she is to be the mother of God's son)
* Luke 1:46–55 (Mary's song of praise)

You will need
* Name sheets for Zechariah, Elizabeth, Gabriel, John, Mary
* Small paper plates; nativity pictures from old Christmas cards cut into rounds to fit on to centre of plates; stars cut from shiny card
* Glue sticks; thread; scissors; sticky tape; pens
* A3 poster with 'With all my heart I praise the Lord, and I am glad because of God my Saviour' at the top
* Large cardboard boxes (possibly painted with white emulsion, optional) and sheets of packing cardboard
* Gaffer or parcel tape
* Candle; matches

Session aim

To know that Mary was willing to listen and do whatever God asked, however difficult it seemed.

Gathering activity

Play 'Simon says' (see Games, page 249) to introduce the theme of listening.

Welcome

Talk about various activities. Is your first response 'Yes, definitely!', 'No way!' or 'Maybe, I'll think about it'?

- Sort the dirty washing.
- Tidy your bedroom.
- Take the rubbish out to the bin.
- Help with the washing up.
- Eat the last chocolate.
- Stop watching TV or using the computer to chat to a visitor.

Ask for suggestions for something we might find it difficult to say 'yes' to straight away.

Ask which Bible people starred in last time's session. Place down the name sheets for Zechariah, Gabriel, Elizabeth and John as they are mentioned. Then add the one for Mary to introduce today's story.

Bible passage

'Don't be afraid,' the angel said
When Mary was startled and raised her head.
'Don't be afraid, God has chosen you
To give birth to his son. Peace be with you!
You will name him Jesus—he'll be God's king.
He'll rule for ever. Will you do this thing?'
'How can it be? I am just a maid.'
'God's power will be on you. Don't be afraid.
Your cousin, Elizabeth, though she's old,
Is having a baby as Zechariah was told.
There is absolutely nothing that God can't do.
Don't be afraid, the Lord is with you!'
'I am his servant,' Mary said.
'Let it be as you say!' and bowed her head.

Mary went to visit her cousin, Elizabeth, who was also expecting a baby. Mary burst into a song of praise. It was a song that talked about the wonder of God.

Ask these questions.
- How was Mary able to say 'yes' when the angel said she would have a special baby?
- Which is the most exciting part of this Bible passage?

Response activities

- **Decoration:** Glue a nativity scene on to the centre of a paper plate, and add a border of shiny stars around the edge of the plate. Make a loop from thread and tape it to the back of the plate so that the decoration can be hung up.
- **Poster:** Add words of praise to the A3 poster.

- **Large-scale:** Create a model of Gabriel by assembling large boxes and sheets of packing cardboard. Secure them with gaffer or parcel tape.
- **Sing:** Learn 'Gloria, gloria in excelsis Deo' (see Resources, page 252). Once the very simple 'Gloria, gloria' has been learned, skip round the room as it is sung. Explain that the words are in Latin and mean 'Glory to God in the highest!' They have been sung for thousands of years. Another song choice could be 'Born in the night, Mary's child' or a carol that children have already learned at school.

Back together

Use the name sheets to think about the different reactions these people had to the angel's message. Ask what the group members would do if Gabriel appeared to ask them to do something extraordinary.

Prayer activity

Light a candle and ask God for courage so that we can do what he wants us to do to make the world a better place. Keep a brief time of silence.

Challenge

Count how many angel decorations can be seen over the following week and remember what Gabriel said to Mary: 'Don't be afraid!'

*

We meet Jesus

God sends good news to the world when Jesus is born. Like
Zechariah and Mary responding to the angel, everyone needs to react
to the birth of Jesus. This session recognises that the world can seem
a dark place, but the light of Jesus shows things differently.

Key Bible verse

Jesus said, 'I am the light for the world! Follow me, and
you won't be walking in the dark. You will have the light
that gives life.'

JOHN 8:12

Bible links

* Isaiah 9:2–7 (light for the people in darkness)

You will need
* Sunglasses; torch
* Picture of people; dark fabric; picture of Jesus in crib
* Black or navy A5 paper folded into three parts
* Sticky label with the words 'Those who walked in the dark'
* Sticky label with the words 'have seen a grear light Isaiah
  9:2'
* Sticky label with the words 'Jesus said, "I am the light for
  the world" John 8:12'
* Shiny paper stars
* Nativity scenes from old Christmas cards
* Pastel crayons; glue sticks
* Selection of toys that change from one thing to another,
  such as Transformers®, nesting dolls or play dough
* Candle; matches
* Dark blankets; torches

Session aim

To know that Jesus brings light into a dark world.

Gathering activity

Play torch tag. One person wears sunglasses and tries to tag others. If they are tagged they must stand still. A second person has a torch, which can 'un-tag' people if it is shone on to their feet.

Give a clear instruction that the torch must not be shone into anyone's eyes, as powerful torches can affect sight.

Welcome

The past two sessions were about Gabriel the angel appearing first to Zechariah, then to Mary. Now, and over Christmas, it is time to think about Jesus, the Son of God, appearing to the world, to us. God, the creator of the universe, became a tiny baby with tiny fingers and toes, lying on his back, looking up at us rather than perhaps looking down on us from heaven. It is topsy-turvy: up and down, dark and light.

Bible passage

Place picture of people.
The people were walking in darkness.

Cover picture with dark fabric.
They had forgotten to look to God.

Raise fabric and shine torch on to picture.
Suddenly they are walking in light.

Add picture of Jesus in crib.
Jesus said, 'I am the light for the world! Follow me, and you won't be walking in the dark. You will have the light that gives life.'

Ask these questions.
• Which is the most important part of the story?
• Is any part of the story about you?

Response activities

• **Tryptych:** Make the A5 paper into three sections by folding the two sides over to meet in the middle. Stick the label saying, 'Those who walked in the dark' on to the front left-hand flap and add drawings of walking people on the right-hand flap.

Open out the folds and stick the label saying, 'have seen a great light Isaiah 9:2' on the inside left section. Add a star. Glue a nativity scene on to the centre section inside and write 'Happy Christmas' underneath. On the inside right section, stick the label saying, 'Jesus said, "I am the light for the world" John 8:12'.

The diagram below shows the finished triptych.

Closed　　　　　　　　　　　　　　Open

- **Toys:** Explore a selection of toys that change from one thing to another.
- **Look:** Sit quietly to listen to God while watching a lit candle burn (this activity must be supervised).
- **Large-scale:** Provide dark blankets (which could be draped over chairs) and torches to explore dark and light.

Back together

December is a dark time of year in the UK, but Christmas is a celebration of Jesus coming to be the light for the world and a light for each person. To live in and by the light of Christ is a choice that everyone can make.

Prayer activity

Spread your dark fabric or blanket in the centre of the group. Talk about some of the dark areas in the world, to which the group would like Jesus to bring his light. Ideas may include places where there is war, famine or persecution; people who are hungry, unhappy, ill or homeless; and people who do not know Jesus as their Saviour. After a number of suggestions have been made, share the torches around the group and explain that the leader will point at each torch holder in turn. As each prayer request is made, one torch will be turned on, to shine on to the cloth and illuminate the prayer. By the end of the prayers, there will be a number of torches shining on to the cloth.

Challenge

Look out for burning candles (including on television) and remember each time that Jesus came to be light for the world, to show everyone a good way to live.

*

Wise people meet Jesus

Tradition says that three wise men, or kings, followed a star to find the newborn king of the Jews. The biblical text does not state that there were three of them, that they were kings or even that they were all men. The important fact is that God called people from other nations, who were not Jews, to worship Jesus. The same call is made today.

Key Bible verse

'Where is the child born to be king of the Jews? We saw his star in the east and have come to worship him.'
MATTHEW 2:2

Bible links

• Matthew 2:1–12 (visitors for Jesus from the east)

You will need
• Large stars cut from white card (see Templates, page 237)
• Glue sticks; pens; glitter
• Teddies (at least six)
• Incense stick, holder and matches
• 24 sheets of A4 paper with instructions written on some, as explained under 'Response activities: large-scale' (see Templates, page 238)
• Masking tape or sticky tack
• One large dice

Session aim

To know that God calls everyone, of whatever background, to worship Jesus.

Gathering activity

Play a game of 'Everyone is called'. Everyone stands around the edge of the space. Call out, 'Come into the centre if you can touch the tip of your nose with your tongue... if you are wearing anything red... if you have a birthday in March... if you like sardines... if you made your own bed today... if you cleaned your teeth this morning... if you are here today!' If people fall into one of the categories announced, they join the growing group in the centre of the space.

Welcome

God calls everyone, wherever they live, whatever their background, and however young or old they are, to worship Jesus. In today's Bible passage some people make a huge effort to visit Jesus.

Bible passage

Encourage everyone to join in the refrain 'Where, oh where?' by practising it at the start.

'Where, oh where is the baby who has been born to be king of the Jews?' asked the wise people who had seen a new star in the sky. They lived in the east, these ever-so-wise people, and they studied the stars.

　　'Where, oh where is this star leading us?' asked the extremely wise people as they set out on a long journey, following the star.

　　'Where, oh where can we find out more about this baby who has been born to be king of the Jews?' asked the exceptionally wise people as they came to Herod's palace.

　　'Where, oh where indeed will the Messiah be born?' demanded Herod of the chief priests and teachers of the Law, when he heard what these visitors from the east wanted. He was not happy.

　　'Where, oh where' pondered the priests and teachers. 'Why, in Bethlehem! That is what the prophet wrote all those years ago.'

Herod summoned the especially wise people and found out about the star they had followed. 'When you have found out **where, oh where** the baby has been born, let me know, so that I can worship him too.'

'Where, oh where has the star reappeared?' wondered the extraordinarily wise people as they went on their way. 'There!' they exclaimed as they saw it over a house.

They went in and found Jesus with his mother, and they knelt down and worshipped him. They gave him special gifts of gold, frankincense and myrrh.

'Where, oh where shall we go as we leave here?' deliberated the enormously wise people. God told them in a dream not to go back to Jerusalem and Herod.

'Where, oh where will this all end?' wondered these extra-wise people.

Response activities

- **Star:** Decorate large card stars with pens and glitter.
- **Retell:** Provide a selection of teddies so that the story of the visitors from the east can be retold.
- **Where, oh where:** Watch a lit incense stick (supervised) while you think about the story.
- **Large-scale:** Create a human-sized board game with a sheet of A4 paper for each 'square'. If the sheets with instructions have been prepared beforehand, the group can help set up the game. The sheets can be secured with masking tape if necessary.

    Leave the first two squares blank. On the third, write, 'See new star—miss one turn'. Leave the next two squares blank and on the sixth write, 'Set out on journey—move forward two spaces'. Provide two more blank squares and on the ninth write, 'Long talk with Herod—go back two'. After two more blank squares, write on the twelfth, 'The king should be born in Bethlehem—move on one'. Provide two more blank squares and write, 'Find star over house—move on one' on the

15th. Provide two more blank spaces and write on the 18th, 'Worship Jesus and give gifts—extra turn'. Two more blank sheets are followed by one saying, 'Stop to sleep—miss one turn'. After two last blank squares, write on the final sheet, 'Return home—mission accomplished'.

Play with a single large dice, each person moving around the 'board' using themselves as the playing piece.

Back together

Talk about the huge number of people who celebrate Christmas around the world. Many people who celebrate do not worship Jesus and do not know him as their friend or brother or guide, but still the story of Christmas is told, year by year.

Prayer activity

Take one of the stars that has been decorated and place it in the centre of the group. Ask how God used the star in today's story.

God of the universe, thank you for making the billions of stars that decorate the sky at night. Help us to think of you when we see their beauty and to praise you.

God of wisdom, thank you for making the special star that guided the wise people to find Jesus. We pray that you will lead lots more people to worship Jesus.

God of power, we pray that you will protect people who want to follow Jesus, especially in countries where being a Christian can be dangerous.

God of love, thank you for caring about every detail of our lives. Please bless each of us and keep us safe this week. Amen

Challenge

Remember to look up at the stars and praise God for something.

Lent

....

The season of Lent is still remembered and even marked by people who neither attend church nor express a Christian faith. It is common to read in newspapers and magazines about people giving up chocolate or alcohol for Lent. For Christians, the weeks leading up to Easter are an opportunity to think about how they live for God. Just as Jesus prepared for his ministry by going into the desert straight after his baptism, so Christians have to train for serving God. Children and adults together need to understand that they can grow as disciples of Jesus—in love for him and in his service towards other people.

A theme song for this series could be 'Jesus, remember me' (see Resources, page 252). The foundational Bible verse for this season, which does not need to be taught, is, 'He stayed there for forty days while Satan tested him. Jesus was with the wild animals, but angels took care of him' (Mark 1:13).

In the first session, one of the response activities suggested is to make a Lenten prayer pot. Small items are then given out at each session, to be placed in the pot as a reminder.

*

Ash Wednesday

Ash Wednesday marks the beginning of Lent, the time of preparation before celebrating Easter. This session introduces the 40 days of preparation (which do not include Sundays) and links them with the 40 days that Jesus spent in the desert, preparing for the work that God had sent him to earth to do.

Key Bible verse

Everything on earth has its own time and its own season.
ECCLESIASTES 3:1

Bible links

* Matthew 4:1–11 (Jesus in the desert)

You will need
* Printed copies of the church year diagram (one for each family if possible) (see Web references, page 243)
* Three dark-coloured sheets of A4 paper; jam jar of silver sand; card with number 40 on it; small stones; bread roll; toy tower; magic wand; small globe or map of world; Bible
* Plasticine® or air-hardening clay; waste paper; wipes
* Sheets with outline of words of Ecclesiastes 3:1 (see Templates, page 239); pens
* Ash from palm crosses (optional)
* Confetti hearts

Session aim

To introduce a time of preparation for Easter that focuses on trying to grow as disciples of Jesus.

Gathering activity

Challenge everyone to stand on one leg for 40 seconds. Then do the same thing, but without smiling or making faces.

Welcome

Ash Wednesday marks the beginning of the 40 days leading up to Easter (not counting Sundays). Show this on the church year diagram. Christians have often used the season of Lent to fast (to abstain from or stop doing something) to help them focus more on God. What sort of things do Christians do to mark Lent? It is more than giving up chocolate or meat or cake. It may be giving more money to charity, spending more time in prayer or reading the Bible, or trying to serve God by helping other people more than usual.

Bible passage

Place three sheets of dark paper end to end to make a long strip from the right to the left of the storyteller. Slowly empty some sand along the length of the paper to make a central strip, again from right to left (so it looks like left to right for those watching), while saying:

After Jesus had been baptised, he went by himself into the desert. He prayed as he prepared to work for God his father. He did not eat for 40 days *(place '40' card at the right of the display)* and he was very hungry. Then Satan, God's enemy, tempted him. He tempted him to do God's work in the wrong way.

Put some stones and a bread roll on to the sand to the left of the '40'.

Satan said, 'You are hungry—and so are lots of people! You could change these stones into bread for yourself and everyone else.' But Jesus answered, 'No! The Bible tells us that we need God's word as much as bread to eat.'

Put the tower and the magic wand to the left of the stones.

Satan said, 'You could prove you are God's Son if you jump off this high tower and don't even get hurt.' 'No!' said Jesus. 'I know from the Bible that I must not put God to the test.'

Put the globe to the left of the tower.

Satan said, 'You could be in charge of all the world so that you could sort everything out—you just have to kneel down and worship me.' 'No!' said Jesus. 'I have learned from the Bible that I must only worship God.'

Place a Bible to the left of the globe to complete the display. Sit back and look slowly at the items from right to left, touching each in turn before resting your hand on the Bible. Pause for at least ten seconds.

Have I put the Bible in the right place in the display? Could we put it anywhere else?

ADAPTED FROM www.barnabasinchurches.org.uk/lent-story-of-jesus-temptations-reflective-story

Response activities

- **Lenten prayer pot:** On a sheet of waste paper, roll Plasticine® or air-hardening clay into a long sausage and use it to make a small coil pot.
- **Bible verse:** Decorate an outline of Ecclesiastes 3:1: 'Everything on earth has its own time and its own season'.

- **Retell:** Use the 'Bible passage' objects to retell the story of Jesus in the desert.
- **Large-scale:** Play hopscotch (see Games, page 247) on a ten-square grid drawn with chalk.

Back together

Explain that, at each session during Lent, everyone will receive a small symbol to help them to think about how they can grow as a disciple (a follower) of Jesus. These symbols can be placed in the Lenten prayer pot or a small box as a reminder.

Prayer activity

If it is the tradition in your church to use ashes on Ash Wednesday, explain how they are made—by burning palm crosses saved from the previous year. Offer to make the sign of the cross, using ash, on the forehead of anyone who wishes to receive one. Ask God to bless each person as they are 'ashed', that they will share God's love in the world.

Otherwise, pray for each person, naming them in turn. Pray that they will grow as disciples of Jesus in the weeks leading up to Easter.

Challenge

Give everyone two small confetti hearts. They can place one in their Lenten pot, if they have made one, or a small box, as a reminder of God's love for them. Encourage them to give the other heart to someone else. Ask for ideas of how to show God's love in the world this week.

*

Waiting on God

Patience is a fruit of the Spirit, and learning to wait for God to guide us or to answer prayer requires patience. There is also something to be learned about not expecting instant answers and solutions but trusting that God will provide in his timing. This is not an easy lesson.

Key Bible verse

I patiently waited, Lord, for you to hear my prayer.
PSALM 40:1

Bible links

* Matthew 25:1–13 (ten lamp-bearers waiting for a wedding)

You will need
* Paintbrushes; runny paint in small pots; coffee filter papers; green pipe cleaners or lengths of floristry wire; newspaper; wipes
* Jenga® bricks, giant or mini
* Pudding basin; plate; flour; 10p coin; dinner knife; tray
* Candle; matches
* Rubber bands

Session aim

To learn that patience is a 'fruit' that comes from the Holy Spirit, but it has to be practised.

Gathering activity

Play 'Sleeping lions' (see Games, page 249), a game that involves waiting.

Welcome

There are still [say number of] days to Easter, which is a long time to wait, for those who have given up chocolate or something else for Lent. Discuss whether giving up sweets, or similar, is the best way to train as a disciple of Jesus. Learn the chorus only of the Taizé chant, 'Wait for the Lord, whose day is near; wait for the Lord: keep watch, take heart' (see Resources, page 252).

Bible passage

Jesus told a story about waiting and being ready when he was talking about the kingdom of heaven.

Ten people (ask for ten volunteers to stand up) were going to meet a bridegroom who was on his way to his wedding. It was dark and the ten people had torches so that they would be able to see where they were going (the ten mime holding a torch). Five of the people (divide the group) were sensible and had brought spare batteries with them (they give a thumbs up), but the other five had not thought ahead (they give a thumbs down) The bridegroom was late, it was nearly midnight and the ten began to fall asleep (they start to lie down).

Suddenly there was a noise as the bridegroom could be heard. The ten shook themselves awake and switched on their torches. The five sensible people were able to put in a new battery if their torch needed it (they give thumbs up). The others found that their torches were going dim (they give thumbs down). They asked to borrow batteries from the others, but they said 'No' (they shake their heads) and told them to go to the shop to buy more (point *away into distance*). So those five set off for the 24-hour shop (*they walk away*).

While they were gone, the bridegroom arrived (*another volunteer enters*). The five who were ready with their torches joined the bridegroom and went into the wedding (*they all move away*). Those who'd had to go shopping came back (*they return*) and called out, 'Let us in!' But the bridegroom called back, 'No! I don't know you!'

Jesus said at the end of his story, 'Always be ready and waiting! You cannot be sure when God will need you to be ready.'

Response activities

- **Flower:** Protect surfaces with newspaper. From a paintbrush, drop small dabs of runny paint on to a filter paper and wait and watch while the colour slowly spreads. Repeat with two more filters. Gather the filters together at the bases and twist a green pipe cleaner around to hold them together and form a stem.
- **Jenga®:** Play Jenga. Everyone waits for the tower to fall as they withdraw a brick at a time.
- **10p drop:** Fill a pudding basin with flour to the brim, and press the flour down. Place a plate on top, turn both over and remove the basin to leave a compacted mound of flour. Balance a 10p coin on top of the mound. Take turns to slice away some flour with a knife. (You may need a tray to catch the flour.) The aim is *not* to be the person who dislodges the coin.
- **Candle:** Sit quietly to watch a lit candle and listen to what God may be saying.

Back together

Discuss why 'waiting for the Lord' may be a good thing.

Prayer activity

Ask the group to suggest some of the really difficult issues in the world that need God's intervention (such as wars, famines, natural disasters or local problems). Explain that each of the issues will be named in turn, and everyone will sing the chorus of the Taizé chant 'Wait for the Lord' between each prayer. Start by practising the chorus.

Challenge

Give everyone a rubber band for their Lenten prayer pot, as a reminder that God stretches his patience and never reaches his limit with anyone. Ask for ideas to help everyone to be more patient this week.

*

The armour of God

Lent is not just about giving up things as a discipline. It can also be a time of taking on more or focusing on spiritual development. This session uses the visual teaching of Paul to think about training for God's service.

Key Bible verse

Let your faith be like a shield.

EPHESIANS 6:16A

Bible links

* Ephesians 6:10–18 (using elements of faith as armour)

You will need
* Church year diagram (see Web references, page 243)
* A child's play suit of armour; large cardboard shields (cut from cereal boxes, with the printing on the back); strips of card; gaffer tape; pens
* Water pistols or pavement chalks
* Tiny shields (shapes or pictures)

Session aim

To understand that being ready to serve God needs training and practice.

Gathering activity

Practise marching in time and in step. Have a 'drill sergeant' to teach everyone to follow the marching instructions. Use lots of 'left–right' and 'by the left, slow march' instructions. Also practise standing to attention with feet together, arms at sides, eyes facing forward and mouths shut.

Welcome

Talk about the marching and ask if people got it right first time. It needs practice! Remind everyone that they are waiting and preparing for Easter during the time of Lent. Show the church year diagram.

Lent is used as a time of preparation, a time of learning how to be a good friend to Jesus and how to serve God. One way that people can think about this is to pretend to be a soldier for God, wearing God's special armour.

Bible passage

Paul, in his letter to the people of Ephesus, advising them on how to live well for God, was thinking about the armour that a soldier wore.

Ask for a suitably-sized volunteer to be dressed in the suit of armour as the passage is read. Pause at the words printed in bold, so that each item can be added before reading on.

Let the mighty strength of the Lord make you strong. Put on all the armour that God gives, so you can defend yourself against the devil's tricks. We are not fighting against humans. We are fighting against forces and authorities and against rulers of darkness and powers in the spiritual world. So put on all the armour that God gives. Then when that evil day comes, you will be able to defend yourself. When the battle is over, you will still be standing firm.

Be ready! Let the truth be like a **belt** around your waist, and let God's justice protect you like a **breastplate**. Your desire to tell the good news about peace should be like **shoes** on your feet. Let your faith be like a **shield**, and you will be able to stop all the flaming arrows of the evil one. Let God's saving power be like a **helmet**, and for a **sword** use God's message that comes from the Spirit.

Never stop praying, especially for others. Always pray by the power of the Spirit. Stay alert and keep praying for God's people.

SLIGHTLY ADAPTED FROM EPHESIANS 6:10–18

Response activities

- **Shield of faith:** Divide the cardboard shields into four quarters and decorate them with symbols of faith (symbols might include a rainbow, a Bible, praying hands, a cross, a fish or a church—but encourage people to choose their own). Use gaffer tape to secure card strips to the back, as handgrips.
- **Drill:** Lead an army-style training session to focus on the different elements of armour. With everyone jogging on the spot, the leader chants each line and the 'squad' repeats it back:

Let the strength of God make you strong.
Put the whole armour of God on.
Let his truth be like a belt:
Round your waist it can be felt.
Put shoes of good news on your feet:
Share the peace of God with all you meet.
Let your faith be like a shield:
It will keep you safe when in the field.
Wear the helmet of God's saving power:
It will keep you safe in your darkest hour.
Use God's message as a mighty sword:
Remember to study God's holy word.
Never stop praying by the Spirit's power,
For everyone needs that blessing shower.
Stay alert and do your drill.
Follow God's way—it is brill.

- **Armour:** Try on the pieces of armour and think about different ways to serve God.
- **Large-scale:** Use water pistols or pavement chalks to draw a soldier wearing the different bits of armour.

Back together

Soldiers spend a lot of their time doing drills to learn how to use their weapons and how to defend themselves. Christians have to put the same effort into learning how to use the word of God in the Bible, to depend on God's help and to share the good news of God's peace.

Prayer activity

Learn the response first (from Ephesians 6:16).

When we feel all on our own
Let our faith be like a shield.
When no one wants to play with us
Let our faith be like a shield.
When people are nasty to us
Let our faith be like a shield.
When we don't know what to do
Let our faith be like a shield.
When we feel scared
Let our faith be like a shield.
When we have to keep going when things are tough
Let our faith be like a shield.
Amen

Challenge

Give everyone a tiny shield to add to their Lenten prayer pot. Ask where the biggest challenge to our use of faith as a shield might come from this week. What things make it difficult to remember how much God loves everyone?

*

Heaven

The words of the third verse of 'Away in a manger' are a prayer asking Jesus to bless us and to 'fit us for heaven to live with thee there'. This session provides everyone with a chance to think about heaven. This links with using Lent as a time of training in discipleship. As we try to follow Jesus more closely, so he is able to 'fit us', to shape us, for heaven.

Key Bible verse

Then Jesus started preaching, 'Turn back to God! The kingdom of heaven will soon be here.'

MATTHEW 4:17

Bible links

- Matthew 13:45–46 (a man looking for pearls)
- Revelation 22:1–5 (the river of life in heaven)

You will need
- A potato
- Stickers saying, 'Jesus loves me'
- A4 paper; pens; pencils; tissue, wrapping or crêpe paper; sequins; glitter glue pens; glue sticks
- Short lengths of pipe cleaner; white beads with a large hole
- Construction toys (Lego®, bricks and so on)
- Long length of fabric, perhaps blue or gold (or colour the reverse of a roll of wallpaper)
- Tiny cards saying 'heaven'

Session aim

To consider the wonders of heaven.

Gathering activity

Play 'Hot potato' (see Games, page 247). Pass the potato round. Whoever is holding the potato when the signal goes (set a three-second reminder on a mobile phone or get a leader to call out 'stop') is invited to stand in the middle. They are told that Jesus loves them and are given a sticker that says so. They then stand outside the group. Repeat until everyone has received their sticker.

Welcome

Explain that the session is about heaven. Take suggestions of what people think heaven might be like. Children and adults may have different views. Jesus often talked about the kingdom of heaven. He thought it was important.

Bible passage

Jesus told his friends lots of little stories—little stories that had a big, big message. This is one of them.

The kingdom of heaven is like a man who is looking for beautiful pearls. He is looking for pearls that glisten, pearls that glow and pearls that are absolutely gorgeous. Wherever he goes, he keeps his eyes wide open. Where will he spot a beautiful pearl? And then it happens! He sees such a pretty pearl, such a precious pearl, such a perfect pearl that he does something exceptional, something extraordinary, something that would take anyone by surprise. He sells all his possessions, everything he has, to have enough money to buy just that one pretty, precious, perfect pearl. That is the value of the kingdom of heaven.

What is Jesus saying in this story? What could be so amazing that you would give up everything you own to get it?

Response activities

- **Heaven:** Make a picture of your idea of heaven (draw it or use collage materials).
- **Ring:** Thread a white bead on to a short length of pipe cleaner to make a 'pearl' ring.
- **Build:** Make a model of some aspect of heaven out of a construction toy.
- **Play:** Take turns to add a describing word for heaven to a list in alphabetical order—for example, 'Heaven is amazing, beautiful, colourful…' and so on.

Back together

Talk about some of the pictures of heaven that have been made. Explain that there is a wonderful word-picture of heaven in the last book of the Bible, Revelation.

Spread a long piece of blue or gold fabric or paper across the centre of the space to represent the river of life (Revelation 22:1). Invite everyone to sit or lie on the 'river' as they listen. Read Revelation 22:1–5:

The angel showed me a river that was crystal clear, and its waters gave life. The river came from the throne where God and the Lamb were seated. Then it flowed down the middle of the city's main street. On each side of the river are trees that grow a different kind of fruit each month of the year. The fruit gives life, and the leaves are used as medicine to heal the nations.

God's curse will no longer be on the people of that city. He and the Lamb will be seated there on their thrones, and its people will worship God and will see him face to face. God's name will be written on the foreheads of the people. Never again will night appear, and no one who lives there will ever need a lamp or the sun. The Lord God will be their light, and they will rule for ever.

Prayer activity

Invite everyone to imagine what heaven may be like—silently, if everyone is in that mood. Otherwise, sing the last verse of 'Away in a manger'. This may be a good occasion to lead everyone in the Lord's Prayer after pointing out the references to heaven in it. Do this by saying one phrase at a time and inviting everyone to repeat it.

Challenge

Jesus said that heaven can be glimpsed now as well as in the future. Where could heaven be glimpsed this week? Challenge everyone to keep a close look-out! Give out a tiny card with the word 'heaven' on it, as a reminder for the Lenten prayer pots.

＊

Towards Easter

Sharing the account of what happened to Jesus, from his procession into Jerusalem, through his last meal with his disciples and his crucifixion and on to his resurrection, in one session helps everyone to understand the sweep of events. Each part of the story is significant and could form the basis of separate sessions, but anyone unfamiliar with the account will benefit from discovering what happened. Using the eight eggs provides a clear sequence for everyone to follow.

Key Bible verse

The man said, 'Don't be alarmed! You are looking for Jesus from Nazareth, who was nailed to a cross. God has raised him to life, and he isn't here. You can see the place where they put his body.'

MARK 16:6

Bible links

- Matthew 21:1–11; 26:17–30, 36–48; 27:27–44, 50–60
- Mark 16:1–6

You will need
- Church year diagram (see Web references, page 243)
- Lenten prayer pot with its contents
- Eight numbered plastic eggs that open with the following contents:
  1: a rolled-up palm cross
  2: a piece of bread
  3: a hand shape cut from paper, or a foam shape
  4: purple fabric

> 5: a small wooden cross
> 6: spices (could be incense-scented hand cream or cooking spices)
> 7: stone
> 8: empty
> • Holy Week and Easter cube net (see Templates, page 240); pens; scissors; glue sticks
> • A4 card folded to make a greetings card
> • Tiny wrapped Easter egg

Session aim

To think about the events of Holy Week and Easter.

Gathering activity

Teach the song below to the tune of 'What shall we do with the drunken sailor?' with actions. For the donkey, pretend to be holding the reins; for the trees, wave arms in the air; for bowl and towel, pretend to hold the bowl in one arm and use the other hand to wipe it out with the towel. 'Sign' Jesus by using the first finger of one hand to point to the palm of the other and then repeat with the opposite hands.

We have a king who rides a donkey (x3) and his name is Jesus.
The trees are waving a royal welcome (x3) for the king called Jesus.
We have a king with a bowl and towel (x3) and his name is Jesus.

Welcome

Our preparation and waiting for Easter are nearly over. Show the church year diagram. Review the different items that have been put into the Lenten prayer pots (heart, rubber band, shield, 'heaven' card). There is one more thing to add later on.

Bible passage

Set the eight eggs where everyone can see them and say that they will be used to explain what happened to Jesus in the last week of his life on earth. After each egg has been opened, leave it and its contents in clear view.

Open the first egg to show the palm cross.

Jesus came to Jerusalem with his friends. Everyone was expecting him to become a king who would lead an army and get rid of the Roman troops. Jesus rode on a donkey, a humble form of transport, as he was not planning to be a soldier-king. The crowd was excitable and people tore down branches from the palm trees to fling in front of the donkey as Jesus rode forward. Some of them even threw their coats down in the road.

Hold the second egg.

Jesus and his friends shared a meal. It was the Passover, a celebration time for the Jews. At the end of the meal *(open the egg and show the bread)*, Jesus broke a piece of bread to share with his friends, and told them to do the same to remember him.

Open the third egg to reveal the hand.

Jesus took his friends outdoors. He wanted to pray and he asked them to pray, too—but they fell asleep. Soldiers came to arrest him.

Hold the fourth egg.

The soldiers jeered at him that he was meant to be the king of the Jews. *(Open the egg to show the fabric.)* They put a purple robe on him. They beat him up.

Open the fifth egg and take out the cross.

Jesus was led outside the city of Jerusalem. He was nailed to a cross and he died. His body was laid in a tomb cut out of the rock. The next day was Saturday, the Jewish sabbath, so nothing happened until early on Sunday morning.

Hold the sixth egg.

Very early in the morning, some of the women who loved Jesus bought some spices so that they could anoint his body.

Open the egg and pass it around for everyone to sniff. (If you are using hand cream, they may wish to take a little to rub on to their hands.)

When the women arrived, they were amazed.

Open the seventh egg to show the stone.

The stone that had been used to block the entrance of the tomb had been rolled away. The women went forward into the tomb.

Open and show the inside of the eighth egg.

The tomb was empty. Jesus had come back to life in a new way. He was not there!

Ask these questions.
- Which egg do you like the best?
- Which egg makes you feel sad?
- Which egg do you want to remember?

Response activities

- **Cube:** Decorate and assemble a Holy Week and Easter cube.
- **Eggs:** Retell the story using the eggs and contents.
- **Mime:** As a group, develop eight movements, based on the eggs, to illustrate the Bible passage.
- **Easter card:** Make an Easter card for someone.

Back together

If anyone has developed the miming movements, ask them to show the rest of the group. Otherwise, ask if anyone has any questions about this part of Jesus' life.

Prayer activity

Lay out the eggs and their contents. Move forward each egg in turn as you pray.

- 1: praise God for sending Jesus to show us how to live.
- 2: thank God for our food.
- 3: ask God to help us pray at all times.
- 4: say sorry for all the times we forget to live as God wants us to.
- 5: keep a few moments of silence as we remember that Jesus died for each of us.
- 6: pray for everyone who is unwell.
- 7: pray for everyone who shares the good news of Jesus with other people.
- 8: rejoice that Jesus, who was dead, is alive now and for ever.

Challenge

Give everyone a tiny wrapped Easter egg to put into their Lenten prayer pot, to keep until Easter Day.

Easter

Many people are not very familiar with the different parts of the Easter story that happened after the resurrection. These three sessions cover Mary Magdalene and two of the disciples discovering the empty tomb, two other followers being surprised by Jesus on the road to Emmaus, and Jesus appearing to seven of his disciples by Lake Tiberias. Together they encourage an understanding that Jesus really did come back to life and that different people talked to him and spent time with him.

The foundational Bible verse for these sessions, which does not need to be taught, is 'Suddenly Jesus met them and greeted them. They went near him, held on to his feet, and worshipped him' (Matthew 28:9). A good song for this series would be the first verse of 'He is Lord, he is Lord' (see Resources, page 252).

Easter morning

Although Jesus had told his disciples that he would come back to life, it seems that they did not expect it to happen. The excitement and confusion that come from the account in John 20 are startling. This session tries to capture some of the energy and uncertainty of that first Easter Day.

Key Bible verse

'Go to my brothers and tell them that I am returning to him who is my Father and their Father, my God and their God.'
JOHN 20:17B (GNB)

Bible links

- John 20:1–17 (excitement at the empty tomb)

You will need
- Small cards saying 'Good News'
- Large plain box or bag; dark-coloured paper; name 'Mary Magdalene' on paper; a stone; a picture of two disciples (search online); white cloth; two small angel figures; toy rake (or picture); word 'Rabboni' on paper; arrow shape (or picture)
- Selection of tissue, crêpe paper, wrapping paper, cotton wool, foil, bubble wrap and other collage materials; thick A4 backing paper
- Glue sticks; scissors; pens or crayons
- Pipe cleaners
- Chalks

Session aim

To understand that people saw Jesus alive after he had been killed.

Gathering activity

Play a 'Good News' relay in two or more teams. Give each team a 'Good News' card. They have to pass their card over the head of the first person, under the legs of the second person, and so on. When the card gets to the last person in the line, that person must run to the front of their team so that the relay can continue.

Welcome

Talk about the excitement of Easter. Acknowledge the delight of Easter eggs and then discuss why eggs are given at Easter (they are a symbol of new life). Easter is a time to celebrate that Jesus came back to life in a new way, after being killed on the cross. This story is a reminder of what happened on the very first Easter Day.

Bible passage

Produce each item from a large plain box or bag, as it occurs in the story. Lay the items down from right to left (so that those watching will see them from left to right).

It was still dark (*dark paper*) on the Sunday morning when Mary Magdalene (*name 'Mary Magdalene'*) went to the tomb where Jesus had been buried. She looked and saw that the stone (*stone*), which had blocked the entrance of the tomb, had been rolled away. Mary Magdalene ran to find Simon Peter and the other disciple, whom Jesus loved (*picture of disciples*). 'They've taken the Lord from the tomb. Where is he?' she said. The two disciples ran to the tomb, and inside they saw the linen wrappings (*white cloth*) that had been used to wrap Jesus' body.

Mary Magdalene *(touch Mary's name)* stood outside the tomb, crying. Then she looked into the tomb again and saw two angels *(angels)*. They asked her why she was crying and she said, 'They have taken Jesus' body away and I don't know where it is.' She looked round and saw someone she thought was the gardener *(rake)*. 'If you've taken the body away, please tell me where you have put it,' she said to the man.

'Mary,' *(touch Mary's name)* said the man.

'Rabboni,' *(word 'Rabboni')* (which means teacher), said Mary, for she suddenly recognised that it was Jesus.

'Go,' said Jesus *(arrow)*. 'Go and tell my disciples that I am going to the one who is my Father and their Father, my God and their God, too.'

Ask these questions.
- Which is the most surprising part of the story?
- Which is your favourite part of the story?

Response activities

- **Collage:** Use colour and texture to record part of the story.
- **Game:** Play a version of 'Fruit salad' (see Games, page 246) to retell the story. Give everyone a name around the circle in turn: Mary, Simon Peter, other disciple, Jesus. Explain that the story will be read again. Whenever a name is mentioned, everyone who has been given that name must get up and run round the circle and back to their place. Point out that when the phrase 'two disciples' is used, both 'Simon Peter' and the 'other disciple' must run round. On the word 'Go', everyone must move.
- **Order:** Use the objects from the Bible passage to retell the story.
- **Arrow:** Use pipe cleaners to shape an arrow as a reminder to 'Go!'

Back together

Ask if anyone who has made a collage would like to talk about what they have made.

Prayer activity

Ask for suggestions of places where the group would want God to bring his light. Use chalks to record the answers on a piece of dark paper. Then place the white cloth as a reminder that Jesus is risen and there is always hope. Finally, place the arrow (pointing away from the white cloth) and ask where God might want to send people in the next few days. Keep a time of silence. End by saying, 'We pray in the name of Jesus who is risen again. Amen.'

Challenge

The last part of the story was about Jesus saying to Mary Magdalene, 'Go!' Take suggestions for how everyone can 'go' in the name of Jesus in the week ahead.

*

Surprised by Jesus

Jesus met a number of his disciples and followers after his resurrection. Some of them recognised him immediately and some did not. The two followers who met Jesus as they walked to Emmaus had no idea who was talking to them. They were blessed to hear Jesus explain all the prophecies in the scriptures about the Messiah, even though they had no idea who this teacher was. They only recognised him when he broke bread and gave thanks to God in a way that was obviously familiar to them.

Key Bible verse

'I will be with you always, to the end of the age.'
MATTHEW 28:20B (GNB)

Bible links

• Luke 24:13–35 (walking to Emmaus)

You will need
• Paper plates
• A4 paper; pens
• One large dice (or several if the group is large)
• Small cards or sheets of paper with a different word on each (walk; talk; Jesus; sad; cross; freedom; angels; Messiah; dark; bread; disappear; joy; Jerusalem)
• Picture of a large question mark

Session aim

To understand that people talked to Jesus after he came back to life.

Gathering activity

Play a game of 'Statues'. Everyone moves around until the leader calls out 'STOP! Gloomy!' Then everyone has to become a statue with a gloomy face and posture. Repeat to make the following statues: joyful; worried; tired; sad; puzzled; wondering.

Welcome

Explain that the season of Easter continues for six weeks. Ask if anyone has any Easter eggs left. The last session looked at the account of Mary Magdalene meeting Jesus in the garden by the tomb where he had been buried, which happened early on the first Easter Sunday morning. Two other people met Jesus later that day, not in Jerusalem but on a dusty road heading out into the countryside.

Bible passage

Invite two people to play the part of Jesus' followers (one named Cleopas) and a third to play Jesus. There needs to be a space in the centre of the group of listeners.

It was the first Easter day and two people *(actors stand up)* were walking from Jerusalem to a village called Emmaus, about seven miles away. *(They walk slowly round the outside of the group.)* They were talking about what had happened to their friend, Jesus—how he had been killed on a cross, and yet the tomb where he had been buried had been found empty that morning. *(Mime talking and looking puzzled.)*

As they walked, they were joined by Jesus *(Jesus walks alongside them)*, but somehow they did not realise who he was. He asked them what they were talking about. They stood still *(actors stop walking)* and looked sad *(sad faces)*. One of them, called Cleopas, told the stranger that he must be the only visitor to Jerusalem who did not know what had been going on. Cleopas explained that Jesus of Nazareth, a prophet and a man really blessed by God, had been sentenced to death on a cross *(Cleopas stretches out his arms as if on a cross)*. He told the stranger that they had hoped that Jesus was going to set the Jewish people free from the Roman soldiers—but Jesus had been killed and now the tomb where he had been buried had been found empty.

Then the stranger began to explain everything about the Messiah that had been written in the scriptures *(Jesus mimes talking and pointing as they all start walking round again)*. As they came to Emmaus, the stranger was about to walk on, but the others asked him to stay, as it was getting dark *(stop walking and have another discussion)*. So they went indoors together and sat down to eat *(move into centre of group to sit down)*.

The stranger took the bread and blessed it *(Jesus pretends to hold up bread, then hands pieces to the others)*. In that moment, the two friends realised that the stranger was Jesus *(Jesus moves out of circle)*, but he had already disappeared.

The friends were filled with joy *(mime happiness)* and decided to hurry back to Jerusalem to tell the eleven disciples what had happened *(move outside circle and walk back round in the opposite direction)*. They found the disciples and told them what had happened on their journey and how they had recognised Jesus *(move into middle of circle and mime telling the story to everyone sitting down)*.

Response activities

- **Faces:** Decorate one side of a paper plate with things that make us sad and the other side with things that make us happy.
- **Storyboard:** Fold a piece of A4 paper in half lengthwise, and then into thirds, to make six equal sections when unfolded. Make six sketches to show what happened on the road to Emmaus.

- **Game:** Everyone stands at one side of the room. The aim is to walk from Jerusalem to Emmaus, on the other side of the room. Each number on the dice allows a different action. Take turns to throw the dice and move as follows.
  - Throw '1': take one pace forward.
  - Throw '2': stand still to chat to companion.
  - Throw '3': take three paces forward as if Jesus had come alongside.
  - Throw '4': stand still, look back and point to Jerusalem.
  - Throw '5': move to other side of room (Emmaus), and wait until a 6 is thrown.
  - Throw '6': move to Emmaus (if not already there) before rushing back to Jerusalem.
- **Retell:** Use the key words on small cards to think about the story of the people walking to Emmaus: walk; talk; Jesus; sad; cross; freedom; angels; Messiah; dark; bread; disappear; joy; Jerusalem. Consider if the words can be used in any other order to tell the same story. This can be done by several people together.

Back together

Learn Matthew 28:20 (GNB) as a memory verse. Chant the verse a couple of times with the emphasis on the syllables shown in bold below. Then form a long line, like a train, and chant it faster, moving along and pumping your arms back and forth like pistons. Add 'Oo-o-oo' for a steam train noise. The chant then becomes, 'Oo-o-oo! Jesus said, 'I **will** be with you **al**ways to the **end** of the **age**.'

Prayer activity

Jesus was able to explain lots of things to the friends who were walking to Emmaus. Place a picture of a large question mark in the centre of the group. Discuss what questions about God or Easter they would like to bring to Jesus in prayer. Summarise some of the questions, then pray:

Lord Jesus, we are puzzled by so many things [name specific queries if appropriate]. *Please send your Holy Spirit to answer some of our questions and to help us understand more about you. Amen*

Challenge

Ask for suggestions of ways to remember that Jesus has promised to be with us always.

*

Breakfast on the beach

Jesus continued to appear to his disciples and followers in the days following his resurrection. None of them was sure if they would see Jesus again and they often seem to have been taken by surprise. In John 21, seven of the disciples (Simon Peter, Thomas, Nathanael, James, John and two others who are not identified) have gone back to fishing. They catch nothing. Once more, they do not immediately recognise Jesus when he calls to them from the beach. Apart from helping them to catch a substantial quantity of fish, Jesus cooks breakfast for them. The cooked breakfast emphasises the physical presence of Jesus as he cares for his friends.

Key Bible verse

Some women in our group surprised us. They had gone to the tomb early in the morning, but did not find the body of Jesus. They came back, saying that they had seen a vision of angels who told them that he is alive.

LUKE 24:22–23

Bible links

• John 21:1–14 (Jesus helps the disciples to catch fish)

You will need
• Garden netting (such as is used to protect strawberries, available from pound shops)
• Strips of plastic from used thin carrier bags (see Web references, page 243)
• Paper; pens; crayons; pencils
• Bread cubes in a basket (with gluten-free alternative if necessary)

Session aim

To know that Jesus continued to care for his disciples.

Gathering activity

Play a game of 'Jesus says' (see 'Simon says' in Games, page 249). Ideas for things that Jesus instructs us to do include: pray; seek to find; put the net on the other side; be still; carry things for each other; be alert and watchful; knock on the door; be joyful. Ideas for instructions without 'Jesus says': be grumpy; stamp feet; sulk; grab; scowl; look worried.

Welcome

Ask what the story was at the last session. Then ask if anyone can remember the challenge and how they got on. Explain that it took the first disciples some time to understand that Jesus had come back to life after he had been killed on the cross and buried. The Bible contains several accounts of the disciples meeting Jesus when he was alive again. Today's story involves fishing, nets and breakfast.

Bible passage

Invite everyone to sit in a long line, behind each other — or in pairs, lined up, if the group is large. Stretch the garden netting down one side of the line.

Imagine you have been following Jesus as he taught and prayed and healed people. You earn your money by fishing on the lake. Today you are confused. You saw Jesus arrested and you saw him killed on the cross. He was dead. Then all sorts of strange things started happening. Some of you went to the tomb and found it empty—and there may have been angels waiting there. Then Jesus just appeared in the room where you had locked yourselves away because you were afraid. Thomas, you were not there, though you got to see Jesus for yourself the following week. Since then, there have been rumours of Jesus being seen, but you are not sure.

Simon Peter said he was going fishing, and you have come along with him. You have fished all night, but you have not caught a single fish. You are tired and fed up.

Suddenly, just as the sun is showing rosy pink as it comes up into the sky, you notice someone standing on the shore of the lake (*point to side of room*). 'What have you caught?' the man asks you. 'Not one fish!' you answer (*invite group to look tired and fed up*). 'Throw your net on to the other side of the boat and then you will find some fish!' he says (*invite group to lift up the net and pass it over their heads to the other side*). Suddenly, the net is so full of fish that it is impossible to pull it into the boat.

One of the disciples realises who the man is and shouts, 'It is the Lord!' (*Invite group to be amazed and delighted.*) Simon Peter (*invite someone to stand up*) jumps into the water and swims for the shore towards Jesus (*Peter pretends to swim*). The rest of you bring the boat and the net full of fish to the shore. Jesus is saying, 'Come and have some breakfast. The fish and the bread are ready.'

You do not know what to think and you do not dare to ask the man if he really is Jesus. This is a very strange morning.

Ask these questions.
- Which is the strangest part of this story?
- Which is the best part of the story?
- Which part of the story do you want to remember?

Response activities

- **Net:** Make a net from strips of carrier bag plastic. Lay one strip down vertically. Knot a second strip to the top end of the first, so that it lies horizontally. Knot another strip to the first, about

10 cm lower down. Continue doing this until you reach the bottom of the first strip. Then lay another strip parallel to the first one, about 10 cm away, and tie all the horizontal strips to this new vertical one. A net of square holes will begin to appear as more strips are added. (*Tip:* It is easier to use different colours for the vertical and horizontal strips. This is an occasion when it is helpful to provide an example of one that has already been made.)

- **Draw:** Draw a scene from the Bible passage.
- **Design:** On paper, design a sandwich with filling as a reminder of this story. Then make the sandwich at home.
- **Re-enact:** Use the garden netting to retell the story.

Back together

Discuss some of the things that have been made. Share any insights that have come from the activities.

Prayer activity

Remind everyone that Jesus gave bread to the disciples on the beach. Say that, in many churches, people share bread and wine as a reminder that Jesus died for them and came back to life in a new way. Explain that, for today's prayer, everyone will have a small piece of bread to eat as they thank Jesus for caring for them. Offer the basket around so that everyone can take a piece, but ask them to wait to eat it until everybody has some. Then eat and pray.

Challenge

Ask for ideas of ways to notice or remember that Jesus is alive during the week.

Ascension, Pentecost and Trinity

The traditional church year follows the accounts of Jesus' appearances after his resurrection by focusing on his ascension into heaven, the dramatic arrival of the Holy Spirit in Jerusalem and then a week of reflection on the Trinity—Father, Son and Holy Spirit together. These sessions make it clear that the story of Jesus continues.

The Peruvian Gloria, 'Glory to God, glory to God' (see Resources, page 252), is an echo song that is easy to learn and sing for this season. This series is underpinned by the following words of Jesus: 'Everything that the Father has is mine. That is why I have said that the Spirit takes my message and tells it to you' (John 16:15). It is not a verse to teach to the group but for the leaders to have in mind as they prepare for each session.

*

Ascension

The account of the ascension, when Jesus was taken into heaven, completes the reports of his life on earth. Jesus talked about going away so that God would send another helper, the Holy Spirit. It may be helpful to show the diagram of the church year to show the sweep of the year from Christmas through Lent to Easter and on, past Ascension to the celebration of Pentecost. If attendance at your group is sporadic, it is a good idea to reinforce the links between different Bible stories and aspects of Jesus' life and the experience of the early church. This session revises the life of Jesus from his birth, through his teaching and healing ministry, to his death and resurrection, before highlighting his reign in heaven at the right hand of God.

Key Bible verse

Jesus answered, 'My kingdom doesn't belong to this world.'
JOHN 18:36A

Bible links

- Matthew 22:44 (Jesus sits at the right hand of God)
- John 16:7 (Jesus says he is going away but God will send the Holy Spirit)
- Acts 1:9 (Jesus is taken up into heaven)

You will need
- Music and music player
- Chairs or sheets of newspaper
- Story bag or box containing: scrap of white cloth, toy sheep, chocolate gold coin, two toy fish, picture of bottle of wine, sticking plaster, small cross, stone, angel and crown

- Life-size crowns cut from thin card; sticky tape; glue sticks; stickers, sequins, feathers, 'jewels', tissue paper and other decorating materials
- Lego® or other construction toy
- Large cardboard boxes; gaffer tape

Session aim

To learn that Jesus went to heaven to reign as king.

Gathering activity

Play 'Musical chairs' (see Games, page 248). Use sheets of newspaper as chairs if space is limited.

Welcome

There is only one winner at the end of 'Musical chairs'. There is only one King Jesus. The Bible tells how Jesus was born and how he showed everyone a good way to live. He was killed on the cross and brought back to life in a new way at Easter. Christians believe that Jesus is still being a friend and teaching wise ways to live. Jesus is also a king, reigning in heaven, right beside God.

Bible passage

Place the story bag or box in the centre of the group and remove an item at a time, as indicated, to display.

Jesus was born in a stable. He was wrapped in cloths *(display cloth)* and laid in a manger. First shepherds *(sheep)* and then wise people *(gold coin)* came to worship him.

Jesus grew to be a man. He called some fishermen (*one fish*) to follow him. The first miracle he did was to turn water into wine (*picture of wine*). He healed people (*sticking plaster*) and he fed them (*another fish*).

In the end, Jesus was killed on a cross (*cross*). He was buried. Some of his friends came to find him, but the stone (*stone*) at the entrance of the tomb had been rolled away. Inside they saw an angel (*angel*) who told them that Jesus had risen from death. His friends saw him alive in a new way, and then they saw him go into heaven to become king (*crown*).

Ask these questions.
- Which is the most important part of the story?
- Can any part of the story be left out without spoiling it?

Response activities

- **Crown:** Decorate a crown suitable for King Jesus.
- **Throne:** Make a throne for Jesus out of Lego® or other construction kit.
- **Large-scale:** Make a life-size throne for Jesus out of large boxes and gaffer tape.
- **Reflect:** Look at the story bag items again.

Back together

Talk about whether Jesus used a crown or a throne when he was living on earth with the disciples. Did people think he was a king then? Why do some churches have a special Sunday to worship Jesus as 'Christ the King'? Discuss whether it is easier to imagine Jesus as a friend or a king.

Prayer activity

Spread out the items from the story bag or box. Ask people to put forward prayers suggested by the different items. For example, the sticking plasters may prompt prayers for people who are unwell. If the group is slow to get started, point to one item at a time and ask what ideas each one gives them for a prayer.

Challenge

Discuss ways to serve Jesus the King over the next few days.

Promise of Pentecost

Before Jesus was killed, when he told the disciples that he would be going away, he promised that God would send another helper or comforter, the Holy Spirit. This session looks at human promises that are so easily broken and at the promises Jesus made and kept. Many families will have experienced the pain that comes from broken promises, so the session can offer hope through Jesus.

Key Bible verse

'I will be with you always, to the end of the age.'
MATTHEW 28:20B (GNB)

Bible links

- John 16:7 (Jesus says that he is going away but God will send the Holy Spirit)

You will need
- £5 note
- C5 envelopes; sets of paper strips, each set showing promises made by Jesus (see pages 112–113)
- Pens; stickers
- Hoops
- Large cardboard boxes or juice cartons
- Silver sand; shallow food trays or similar

Session aim

To emphasise that God keeps his promises.

Gathering activity

Play a version of 'Grandma's shopping game' (see Games, page 246). The first person promises to do something every day—for example, 'I promise to clean my teeth every day.' The next person has to add something to the first statement, such as, 'I promise to clean my teeth and make my bed every day.' The third person repeats the first two promises and adds another. Leaders could encourage the inclusion of some silly ideas, such as, 'I promise to pat my head each time I have a drink.'

Welcome

Show a £5 note. Apart from its value, what other important thing is written on the note? The promise! Discuss who makes promises (Brownies and Cub Scouts, people getting married, parents, children, the government, shops and so on). Debate whether promises are always kept, and whether it is possible always to keep a promise. Discuss why keeping promises is so difficult.

Bible passage

Jesus made lots of promises. Ask if anyone can think of some. From an envelope, take out one slip of paper at a time, read aloud the promise of Jesus written on it and place it on display (see 'Response activity' below). Invite comments and discussion on each one.

Jesus promised, 'I will be with you always' (Matthew 28:20).

Jesus promised, 'The Holy Spirit will come and help you, because the Father will send the Spirit to take my place. The Spirit will teach you everything and will remind you of what I said while I was with you' (John 14:26).

> Jesus promised, 'I give you peace, the kind of peace that only I can give. It isn't like the peace that this world can give. So don't be worried or afraid' (John 14:27).

> Jesus promised, 'I am the way, the truth, and the life' (John 14:6).

> Jesus promised, 'There are many rooms in my Father's house... I am going there to prepare a place for each of you. After I have done this, I will come back and take you with me. Then we will be together' (John 14:2–3).

> Jesus promised, 'If you are tired from carrying heavy burdens, come to me and I will give you rest. Learn from me... and you will find rest' (Matthew 11:28–29).

Response activities

- **Envelope:** Decorate the outside of an envelope with drawings and stickers. Add slips of paper with Bible verses that show Jesus' promises.
- **Game:** Play 'Hoop promise' (see Games, page 247).
- **Large-scale:** Build a 'promise tower' of boxes or juice cartons. Find out what happens if one of the promises, low down in the tower, is broken (that is, removed).
- **Sand:** Doodle in a small sand tray and think about the promises that Jesus made.

Back together

People do not always manage to keep promises—but Jesus did, because he is the only perfect person ever to have lived. After Jesus had been killed and had come back to life in a new way, but before he went into heaven, he said: 'I have been given all authority in heaven and on earth! Go to the people of all nations and make them my disciples. Baptise them in the name of the Father, the Son, and the Holy Spirit, and teach them to do everything I have told you. I will be with you always, even until the end of the world' (Matthew 28:18–20).

Prayer activity

Lay the £5 note and the slips of paper with Jesus' promises in the centre of the group. Pray that everyone will remember that Jesus keeps his promises. Ask God to help everyone keep the promises they make.

Challenge

Discuss which would be particularly good promises to keep. Share ideas for ways of keeping them.

Pentecost

When the power of the Holy Spirit came upon the first disciples, their lives were changed. Instead of meeting with the other believers indoors, to pray and talk about the resurrection, Peter found himself addressing a huge crowd. He was able to explain that Jesus was the Messiah, the descendant of David whom everyone had been waiting for. He spoke so powerfully that 3000 people were added to the group of believers that day. The Holy Spirit brings joy and love with his power, so this is a session of celebration.

Key Bible verse

'I am the way, the truth, and the life!' Jesus answered. 'Without me, no one can go to the Father.'

JOHN 14:6

Bible links

- Acts 2:1–4 (the Holy Spirit comes at Pentecost)

You will need

- 3-metre length of thin metre-wide fabric (or a small parachute); lengths of wide ribbon (optional)
- Kite or windsock
- Red handkerchief, thin scarf or ribbon
- Plain badges (or discs of card with a safety pin taped to the back); red, orange and yellow crêpe or tissue paper; glue sticks; pens
- White household candles; liquid wax candle-decorating pens (see Web references, page 243)
- Words and music for 'We are marching'
- Praise flags or ribbons (optional); percussion instruments or noise makers

Session aim

To celebrate the power and joy of Pentecost.

Gathering activity

Shake pieces of thin fabric (or small parachute) and pieces of wide ribbon, if using, to send ripples along their length.

Welcome

Display a kite or windsock. Talk about what is needed for the kite to be exciting and good to use.

Bible passage

Practise making the sound of a quiet wind (shhh) and then a strong wind (whoosh).

The disciples were all together. They had watched Jesus go away into heaven. Jesus had told them to wait in Jerusalem. They were not sure what they were waiting for, but they came together to pray.

It was the day of Pentecost, a Jewish festival. Suddenly the disciples heard the sound of wind. It was not a quiet wind *(shhh)*. No, it was a strong wind *(whoosh)* that the disciples heard. *(Whoosh)* It blew right through the house where they were meeting together. *(Whoosh)* It seemed to fill the whole house—not a quiet wind *(shhh)* but a strong one *(whoosh)*.

Then something else strange happened. *(Move round the group, touching heads with a red handkerchief, scarf or ribbon.)* There seemed to be tongues of fire resting on each of them. Suddenly the disciples were filled with power. *(Invite everyone to make a 'strong' body shape.)* They began to speak in other, foreign languages.

Ask these questions.
- What is surprising about this Bible story?
- What is most exciting about it?

Response activities

- **Badge:** Decorate a badge with pens, and add paper flames (a symbol of the Holy Spirit) around the edge.
- **Candle:** Use liquid wax pens to add flame shapes to the sides of a plain candle.
- **Song:** Play and sing the song 'We are marching in the light of God'.
- **Large-scale:** Play with the large piece of fabric or parachute, lifting it up to catch the air.

Back together

Explain that it was exciting when the Holy Spirit came to the disciples, and God wants to send his Holy Spirit today. If the song 'We are marching' has been learned, arrange a lively procession with everyone marching, dancing or playing instruments. Use praise flags or ribbons and percussion instruments, if you have them.

Prayer activity

Ask four people to hold the corner of the large piece of fabric or parachute. Invite each person in turn to walk under the fabric as it is wafted into the air and the leader prays, 'Holy Spirit, bless [name].' Make sure the four lifters are given their turn, too.

Challenge

Watch for the wind blowing the leaves of a tree or bush and thank God for sending his Holy Spirit into the world.

*

Trinity

In Genesis 1, the very beginning of the Bible, God creates the universe with his Word (Jesus), as his Spirit broods over the ocean. The opening of John's Gospel also emphasises that the Word was with God and was God at the start of everything.

Key Bible verse

Jesus said, 'Everything that the Father has is mine. That is why I have said that the Spirit takes my message and tells it to you.'
JOHN 16:15

Bible links

- John 16:1–15 (Jesus promises that the Spirit will reveal the truth about God)
- Romans 5:1–5 (peace with God through Jesus, and the gift of his Holy Spirit)

You will need
- A3 paper; pens
- Words and music for 'Father, we adore you'
- Lengths of wool (22–25 cm) in different colours
- Cardboard tubes from kitchen roll, with prayer categories written on them (see page 121); tennis or other light ball

Session aim

To learn more about God as Father, Son and Holy Spirit.

Gathering activity

Form groups of three people, linking arms if they all belong in the categories announced. Possible categories are: having a 'J' in your first name; wearing red; having a 6 in your age; born *not* in England; wearing size 3 shoes; wearing earrings; birthday in March; God loves you (everyone!). Adapt these categories according to your knowledge of the group.

Welcome

This session is about thinking in threes, as it is the church season of Trinity. Christians know God as their Father, God as Jesus his Son and their Saviour, and God as the Holy Spirit who guides them. Invite everyone to close their eyes and imagine as they listen to the Bible passage.

Bible passage

Jesus was talking to his special friends. He knew that he would soon be arrested and put to death on a cross. He had spent three years talking to them about God his Father, telling them good ways to live and explaining the scriptures they had heard in the synagogue since they were small. He was warning them to stay true to what he had taught them, to love one another and be ready to be mistreated by the authorities. Listen to what Jesus said to his disciples.

'The Spirit shows what is true and will come and guide you into the full truth. The Spirit doesn't speak on his own. He will tell you only what he has heard from me, and he will let you know what is going to happen. The Spirit will bring glory to me by taking my message and telling it to you. Everything that the Father has is mine. That is why I have said that the Spirit takes my message and tells it to you' (John 16:13–15).

Ask these questions.

- What picture came into your head as you listened to what Jesus said?
- What would you have said to Jesus if you had been there with his special friends?

Response activities

- **Triples:** Together, think of sets of three words beginning with the same letter that describe God—for example, magnificent, mega and mighty; or kind, kingly and knowing. Talk about the choices. Record them as a poster on A3 paper.
- **Song:** Learn the three verses of 'Father, we adore you'. This can be sung as a round once everyone is secure with the tune.
- **Wristband:** Plait three lengths of wool together with a knot at each end. Tie around your wrist.
- **Large-scale:** Form a human equilateral triangle using bodies lying on the floor. It may be necessary to have one adult and one small child on one side to balance three small children on another side. Experiment to find a solution.

Back together

Teach, then sing, the three verses of 'Father, we adore you' (see Resources, page 252) if not already learned. If a group of people have learned the song as a response activity, they can lead the singing now.

Prayer activity

Play 'Prayer skittles'. Set up cardboard tubes with the following categories written on them:

- Father God, please
- Father God, sorry

- Father God, thank you
- Holy Spirit, show us
- Holy Spirit, help us
- Holy Spirit, tell us
- Jesus, look after
- Jesus, teach us
- Jesus, you are

Take turns to bowl down the skittles. When any are knocked down, ask for suggestions to pray those categories. Keep going until all the skittles have been knocked over. Repeat as required.

Challenge

Suggest that people either wear their wristband as a reminder of the love of God the Father, God the Son and God the Holy Spirit, or take one of the prayer skittles as a reminder to pray.

Jesus

Jesus showed his disciples, and us, who he was through his words and actions. He was a teacher, a friend, a healer and a worker of miracles when he lived on earth. He was known for his wisdom and his kindness. This series shows these different aspects of his life and work.

Everyone has to answer, for themselves, the same question that Jesus asked his first disciples: 'But who do you say I am?' (Matthew 16:15). This is the main verse that underlies this series but it does not need to be taught as a memory verse. A good theme song would be 'Jesus, you're my superhero' (see Resources, page 252).

✳

Jesus the teacher (1)

Jesus told stories to challenge people to think in new ways. In the parable of the greedy farmer, he says that lots of money or things do not make people well-off in God's view. There is an opportunity in this session to think about starting a social action project. Such projects help all ages to realise how well-off they are compared with many other people and to understand that they can make a difference. Taking part in social action, 'being Jesus in the world', is a significant part of growing as a disciple of Christ.

Key Bible verse

I will give thanks to you, Lord, with all my heart; I will tell of your wonderful deeds.

PSALM 9:1 (PARAPHRASED)

Bible links

- Luke 12:15–21 (a greedy farmer)

You will need
- Kitchen roll; pencils; fibreboard or coated paper plates; plastic bottle of water; cress seeds
- Empty plastic water or sports drink bottles (with necks wide enough to receive 1p and 5p coins); stickers
- Water pistols

Session aim

To recognise all the blessings God gives and to understand the need to thank him.

Gathering activity

Give the following instructions.

- Move to the side of the room if you have eaten dessert, pudding or chocolate this week; stand in the middle if you have not. (Explain that people who don't have enough food rarely get dessert.)
- Move to the side if you can drink water many times a day; stand in the middle if you can't. (Some people are hungry because they have no water to make their crops grow.)
- Move to the side if your freezer at home has bags or boxes of food in it; stand in the middle if not. (Many people do not have refrigerators or freezers to keep food fresh.)
- Move to the side if you have to walk a mile to get a drink of water; stand in the middle if you can get it out of a tap. (In many countries, people walk a long way to get water, which may be dirty anyway.)
- Move to the side if you ate meat or fish yesterday; stand in the middle if you didn't. (Many people eat only grains and very little protein; they may never get to eat fish or meat.)

Welcome

Most people in this country have a lot to thank God for: food, clean water, lots of stuff, holidays and days out. Are all these things essential? There is so much to thank God for. Jesus often talks about the importance of giving thanks and not being greedy for more than is needed.

There is a lovely verse of a psalm, written more than 3000 years ago, which helps us to focus our attention on God. To teach this memory verse, chant it in waltz time, with the stress on the syllables in bold:

'I'll give **thanks** to you, **Lord**, with **all** my **heart**; I will **tell** of your **won**derful **deeds**' (Psalm 9:1).

Bible passage

Jesus told this story to tell everyone that life is not all about what people own or how rich they are.

There was a rich man who owned some land that grew very good crops. The rich man with the land that grew such very good crops found himself with a problem. It was a problem that was getting bigger as the land grew more and more very good crops. The rich man who owned the land did not have enough barns to store the very good crops that his land grew.

The rich man made a decision: 'I own enough land to pull down the barns that I already have, to build vast warehouses to store the very good crops that my land grows—as well as everything else that I own. That is my plan, for I am a lucky man, as well as being rich and owning land that grows very good crops. I will have all the good things I need to live a lovely life for years and years to come.'

But God saw things differently. 'You are an idiot,' he said to the rich man with the foolish plan. 'This very night you will lose your life—and lose all these things you have stashed away for yourself. When you are dead, who will get all your stuff?'

Jesus said, 'You may be rich by the world's standards, but you are not rich in God's view.'

Ask these questions.
- What did God think was wrong with the man's plan?
- What makes people rich in God's view?

Response activities

- **Thanks:** Use a pencil to write 'thanks' lightly on to a sheet of kitchen roll. Place the sheet on top of another sheet of kitchen roll on a fibreboard or paper plate. Dampen the paper with water from a plastic bottle. Thinly sprinkle cress seeds over the 'thanks' outline.

- **Save:** Make an empty water or sports drink bottle into a savings bank for a good cause. Talk about which cause to support (there may be a link with the 'Share' activity below). Decorate the bottle with stickers and save 1p and 5p coins in it.
- **Large-scale:** Use water pistols to draw ever larger storehouses. The challenge is to see how many storehouse outlines can be drawn in a given space, starting with the smallest barn.
- **Share:** Plan a way to share some of the wealth in the group with people who have much less. Ideas to consider might be supporting a local foodbank or drop-in centre; collecting money to fund a clean water project; organising a tea party for people living on their own or looking after a family member with disabilities; or making birthday cakes for children in need.

Back together

Hear from groups that have been talking about saving money to give away or finding other ways to support people in need. If you are choosing a cause to support, a vote may be necessary to come to agreement. Point out that serving other people like this can be a way of saying 'thank you' to God for all his blessings. Practise the memory verse again.

Prayer activity

Ask what people want to thank God for. After each suggestion, say the memory verse together.

Challenge

Start filling the savings bottles with 1p or 5p coins, or keep the cress seeds watered until they can be eaten.

*

Jesus the teacher (2)

Jesus taught with authority. He taught that his words and instructions are the correct way to live—looking after people in need, not being greedy, not judging others, and asking God for the things we need. This session highlights the importance of basing our lives on his teaching.

Key Bible verse

'Anyone who hears and obeys these teachings of mine is like a wise person who built a house on solid rock.'
MATTHEW 7:24

Bible links

- Matthew 7:24–27 (two house builders)
- Luke 10:5 (sharing God's peace)

You will need
- Large outline of a house drawn on paper, with room for words to be written underneath; sticky notes
- 'Peace' sign or card
- Packs of playing cards; cushions
- Templates for a 3D house, printed on thin card (see Web references, page 244); pens; scissors; glue sticks; sticky tape
- Large cardboard boxes
- Sand in a large bowl or sandpit; a flat stone; model houses (could be made from Lego®)

Session aim

To understand that Jesus said it is wise to follow his teaching.

Gathering activity

Ask each person to draw a tiny self-portrait or write their name inside a large outline of a house. It may be easiest to do this on individual sticky notes, which can then be added to the main picture.

Welcome

Explain that Jesus wanted everyone to share God's peace with each other. Pass a 'peace' sign or card around the group. For each person, say 'May God's peace be with [name]' as they hold the sign.

Bible passage

Teach a hand jive to accompany the chorus: two 'building' move-ments, fist on fist; two 'flat hands' movements, one over the other; two thumbs over shoulders; a hand roll.

You wanna hear a story? It's a-old and it's good
And it's told by a man who's a real cool dude.
So pin back your ears, stop picking your nose
And join in the rhythm, 'cos the rhythm goes:

You gotta build, build, build, build on the rock… the rock…
the rockety rock.

Yeah Jesus said, 'If you hear what I say
And if you live your life [two claps] my way
You're just like the man thinking, 'Where shall I live?'
And when you ask him, here's the answer he'll give:

You gotta build, build, build, build on the rock... the rock...
the rockety rock.

So the man sets to work and he digs down deep
And his sweat pours down from his hat to his feet
But he goes on digging till the job is through,
And if you ask why, then he'll tell you:

You gotta build, build, build, build on the rock... the rock...
the rockety rock.

So he builds his house right there on the rock
Slowly, strongly, block by block
And when the storm comes with the wind and the rain
His house stands firm and he says it again:

You gotta build, build, build, build on the rock... the rock...
the rockety rock.

But if you hear the words of God
And live your life ignoring the lot
You're just like the man who did his own thing
He just laughed when they said to him:

You gotta build, build, build, build on the rock... the rock...
the rockety rock.

No, this man chose to build on the sand
At first it went just as he planned
The sand was soft and a-easy to dig
And in no time at all, his house grew big.

You gotta build, build, build, build on the rock... the rock...
the rockety rock.

'What? Build on the rock when it's hard?' he said
'No thanks!' he yelled and he went to bed
'Look at my house! It's easy and cheap
Who in their right mind wants to dig down deep?'

You gotta build, build, build, build on the rock… the rock…
the rockety rock.

But what do you know? It started to rain
And the wind it blew again and again
And the waters rose with a splosh and a splash
And the house on the sand collapsed with a great and enormous and
ear-splitting CRASH!

And the first man probably sighed
and opened his door
and welcomed in the very wet and soggy silly second man
and said quietly, 'Next time…

You gotta build, build, build, build on the rock… the rock…
the rockety rock.' Yeah.
© Lucy Moore, www.barnabasinchurches.org.uk/house-on-the-rock-rap/

Response activities

- **Cards:** Build houses out of playing cards. Repeat using a cushion as a base.
- **Tiny:** Cut out, decorate and assemble a tiny house (see Web references for a template, page 244).
- **Large-scale:** Build a huge house out of large boxes.
- **Retell:** Provide sand, a flat stone and model houses to explore the story.

Back together

Talk about the difficulties of building a secure house using different methods. Ask why Jesus told the story of the two house builders. Discuss why it is important to live the way Jesus taught.

Prayer activity

Ask for some examples of what Jesus said were good ways to live. Write them under the large house outline as part of the 'foundations'. Pray for everyone whose portrait or name appears in the house *(point at each one for a moment)* to live on the solid foundation of Jesus's teaching *(slowly point at the words making up the foundation of the house)*.

Challenge

Invite everyone to choose one of the 'foundation' words or phrases to try to follow during the week.

*

Jesus the friend (1)

The Bible makes it clear that God knows each of us by name. Jesus calls the man lowered through the roof 'my friend' as he forgives his sins (Luke 5:20) and he addresses the disciples as 'friends' (John 15:14–15). Most people find it helpful to think about Jesus as a friend and brother, not just a remote historical figure.

Key Bible verse

I have called you by name; now you belong to me.
ISAIAH 43:1B

Bible links

* John 1:43–50 (Jesus calls Philip and Nathanael)

You will need
* Fresh or dried figs, cut into pieces to taste (or fig roll biscuits)
* Paper; pens
* Small figures to represent Jesus, Philip and Nathanael; small model tree
* Outline of a tree drawn on large paper; scissors; pencils; brown and green paper; glue sticks
* Thin A4 card

Session aim

To understand that everyone can be a friend of Jesus, as he knows our names.

Gathering activity

Play 'Human dominoes' (see Games, page 247).

Welcome

Show some pieces of fig or fig rolls and then offer them to everyone to eat.

Make a list of all the people who know everyone in a particular group by name (parents, family, teachers, friends, neighbours, doctors and so on). What does it feel like if a stranger suddenly calls you by name?

Bible passage

Jesus decided to go to Galilee (show 'Jesus' figure). He found Philip (add 'Philip' figure) and said, 'Come with me!' Philip decided that, yes, he would go with Jesus, but first he went to find his friend, Nathanael. (Move Philip next to 'Nathanael' figure sitting under the tree). Philip was excited and said to Nathanael, 'We've found the person Moses and the prophets wrote about all those years ago!'

'Mmm... right,' replied Nathanael.

'Yes, really! He's called Jesus and he is the son of Joseph—from Nazareth!'

'Nazareth?' scoffed Nathanael. 'Can anything good come out of Nazareth?' He was not from Nazareth himself and had a very low opinion of the place.

'Just come and see,' retorted Philip. (Move Philip and Nathanael next to Jesus.)

Jesus noticed them coming towards him and said, 'Here is a true Israelite—there is nothing crooked about him!'

'What?' exclaimed Nathanael. 'How do you know me?'

'I saw you sitting under the fig tree before Philip invited you along.'

'Hey, Teacher! Respect! You are the Son of God; you are the King of Israel!'

'Are you saying that just because I told you I saw you sitting under the fig tree? asked Jesus. 'You haven't seen anything yet! You come with me.'

Ask these questions.
- What is most surprising about this story?
- Which person in the story is most like you?

Response activities

- **Display:** Provide the outline of a tree drawn on large paper. Draw around your own hand on to green paper, add your own name to the hand shape and glue it to the top of the tree to create the effect of foliage. Then, as a group, glue on torn pieces of brown paper to create a gnarled trunk.
- **Invitation:** Using thin A4 card, make an invitation card to ask someone to 'come and see' a session of your group.
- **Retell:** Use the people figures and the tree to retell the story.
- **Game:** Sit in a circle. Going round the group, label the first person 'Jesus', the second 'Philip' and the third 'Nathanael'. Repeat until everyone has one of these three labels. Retell the story. Every time one of the names is mentioned, everyone who has that label must run around the outside of the circle until they find another empty place to sit in.

Back together

What happened to Nathanael? The Bible says that he was one of the disciples who went fishing with Peter after Jesus had been killed and come back to life in a new way. He shared the breakfast that Jesus cooked for them. Nathanael was one of the first people Jesus asked to follow him. He was very doubtful, but he became a real follower of Jesus.

Prayer activity

Gather round the tree display. Thank God for each of the people named and all the others who have come along. Ask God to show the group new people to invite along, and pray for everyone to understand they can be a friend of Jesus.

Another way to pray would be to teach the famous part of the Prayer of Richard of Chichester:

O most merciful Redeemer, Friend, and Brother,
May I see you more clearly,
Love you more dearly,
And follow you more nearly,
Day by day.

Challenge

Talk about how Philip invited his friend to meet Jesus. Encourage everyone to think of a friend who might like to receive an invitation to meet Jesus. Invite someone to come to the next session.

*

Jesus the friend (2)

Jesus wanted to share the good news of God with everyone. When he saw how interested Zacchaeus was to see him (climbing a tree for a good view was exceptional behaviour), he responded with delight. Jesus looked beyond the man's reputation as a tax collector. Zacchaeus would have been shunned by the other Jews because he collaborated with the Roman authorities. Jesus saw Zacchaeus as someone who was 'lost' and who could be brought back into the community.

Key Bible verse

Jesus looked up and said, 'Zacchaeus, hurry down! I want to stay with you today.'
LUKE 19:5

Bible links

- Luke 19:1–10 (the story of Zacchaeus)

You will need
- Small stepladder or chair
- Cardboard tubes from kitchen roll; lengths of green crêpe paper (20 cm x 4 cm); glue sticks; letter 'Z's (about 4 cm square) cut from white card; sticky tack
- Pens; A4 paper; selection of paper, fabric and collage scraps
- People figures
- Candles; matches
- Lolly sticks or wooden craft sticks

Session aim

To understand that God's kingdom is for everyone.

Gathering activity

Play 'Who's welcome?' (see Games, page 249).

Welcome

In the game, by the end, everyone was able to take part; everyone was invited to join in. Jesus invites everyone to be part of the kingdom of heaven. That is what Zacchaeus found out.

Bible passage

Choose one person to be Jesus and one to be Zacchaeus, and ask the rest to play the part of the crowd. Ask everyone except Jesus to mill around in the centre of the space.

Jesus was on his way to Jerusalem, and he was passing through the town of Jericho. Everyone wanted to see Jesus. Zacchaeus wanted to see Jesus, but he knew he did not stand a chance because he was not very tall. He was rich because he was a tax collector, but he was not tall. Zacchaeus noticed a tree and so he climbed it to get a better view.

Zacchaeus climbs a small stepladder or on to a chair.

Jesus came through the crowd.

Get the crowd to part so that Jesus can walk through, towards Zacchaeus.

Jesus looked up and saw Zacchaeus in the tree. 'Come straight down, Zach! I need to stay in your house today.'

Zacchaeus climbs down.

Zacchaeus nearly fell down the tree in his amazement, but he quickly took Jesus with him into his house. He was delighted to welcome this amazing person he had heard so much about.

Zacchaeus and Jesus move to one side. The crowd grumble.

The crowd said, 'This cannot be right. Jesus has gone into the house of a sinner. Zacchaeus is a tax collector and he has cheated us out of our money.'

Zacchaeus heard what they were saying and he knew it was true. He had not been honest. He turned to Jesus and said, 'I know I have done bad things. I will put things right. I will give half of all my stuff to poor people. What is more, if I have cheated anyone I will pay them back four times as much.'

Jesus smiled as he said, 'Today, Zach has come back into the fold. That is why I am here!'

Ask these questions.
- What is the strangest part of this story?
- Why do you think Jesus was so delighted that Zacchaeus promised to put things right?

Response activities

- **Tree:** Use a cardboard tube as the trunk of a tree. Glue lengths of green crêpe paper into the top of the tube so that they fan out like leaves. Decorate the 'Z' (which represents Zacchaeus). This can then be attached to either the top or bottom of the tree with sticky tack and moved about.

- **Collage:** Illustrate part of the story.
- **Re-act:** Read through the story again with everyone miming the actions of every person.
- **Retell:** Provide people figures, so that the story can be retold.

Back together

Look at some of the artwork produced. Demonstrate how the 'Z' can be moved up and down the tree. Remind everyone how excited Zacchaeus was to be greeted by Jesus and to become his friend.

Prayer activity

Light a candle to encourage everyone to sit quietly. Invite them to think about their own friends, the people they like to spend time or play with. There are lots of people they do not choose to play with. That is not how God does things. Jesus would like everyone to be aware of people who are not their friends and find ways to be friendly.

Keep a few moments of silence, then say the Prayer of Richard of Chichester, as in the previous session.

O most merciful Redeemer, Friend, and Brother,
May I see you more clearly,
Love you more dearly,
And follow you more nearly,
Day by day.

Challenge

Every day, pray for someone who is not your particular friend, by name. Take a lolly stick and write the name of the person on it. Add a little decoration to the stick every time you pray for that person.

*

Jesus the healer

When Jesus promised to give 'life in its fullest' (John 10:10), he was talking about physical and mental health as well as emotional and spiritual well-being. In the Gospels, there are many accounts of Jesus healing people in different ways. In today's story, Jesus recognises the faith of the friends and their commitment in bringing the paralysed man to him.

Key Bible verse

Jesus… healed every kind of disease and sickness.
MATTHEW 4:23

Bible links

* Mark 2:1–12 (Jesus heals a paralysed man)

You will need
* A4 paper; pens
* Two towels; two soft toys
* Lengths of rope, thick string or wool
* Lego® or other construction kit
* Large sheet of paper divided into 4-cm squares

Session aim

To understand that Jesus heals people who are unwell.

Gathering activity

Get everyone involved in tying together lengths of rope, string or wool. Make sure the children are carefully supervised.

Welcome

Discuss whether the short lengths of rope or string become more useful when they are tied together. Ask what other things are better when they are joined together. (Suggestions might include building bricks, cake ingredients and people to push a car.)

Bible passage

This Bible story is about Jesus, four faithful friends and a roof. Practise the actions so that everyone is ready to react when they hear the phrases.

- Paralysed man: lie still on the floor
- Crowds: shuffle together, squashed up
- Friends: link arms in groups of four
- Teachers of the Law: sit cross-legged on the floor, stroking imaginary beards
- Jesus: stand tall, arms reaching out

A long time ago, there was a man who was paralysed (*lie on floor*). He could move neither his arms nor his legs. Life was not good, but he had four faithful friends (*link arms in groups of four*). His faithful friends wanted to do something to help the paralysed man (*lie on floor*) and so the four faithful friends (*link arms*) came up with a plan.

They had heard that Jesus (*stand tall, arms reaching out*) was in their village. The four faithful friends (*link arms*) decided to carry the paralysed man (*lie on floor*) to see Jesus (*stand tall*).

When the four faithful friends (*link arms*) reached the house where Jesus was talking to everyone (*stand tall*), they found that it was full, with a crowd of people (*shuffle together, squashed up*). In fact, the four faithful friends (*link arms*) found that it was impossible to get the paralysed man (*lie on floor*) into the house because of the crowds of people (*shuffle together*).

The four faithful friends (*link arms*) were so desperate to get the paralysed man (*lie on floor*) to see Jesus (*stand tall*) that they carried him up on to the roof. They tore away at the branches and mud that made up the roof, then they carefully lowered the paralysed man (*lie on floor*) down through the crowds (*shuffle together*) until he was in front of Jesus (*stand tall*).

Jesus spoke to the paralysed man (*lie on floor*) and said, 'Go! Your sins are forgiven!' The teachers of the law (*sit cross-legged and stroke imaginary beards*) were shocked. Only God could forgive sins. But Jesus (*stand tall*) knew what the teachers of the law (*sit cross-legged*) were thinking. 'Is it easier to forgive this man's sin's or make him walk?' Jesus (*stand tall*) asked the teachers of the law (*sit cross-legged*). Then Jesus (*stand tall*) spoke to the paralysed man (*lie on floor*): 'Stand up, pick up your mat and walk home!' And he did so!

The four faithful friends (*link arms*) were delighted and the crowds (*shuffle together*) were amazed. Everyone praised God for the wonderful miracle of healing they had seen.

Ask these questions.
- What was most surprising about this story?
- Who would you like to be in this story?

Response activities

- **Get well card:** Fold a piece of A4 paper in half to make a card to give to someone who is unwell.
- **Race:** Divide into two teams. Four people each hold a corner of a towel on which a soft toy is balanced. At the signal, they carry the soft toy to the other side of the room and return. The next four then repeat the lap. If there are not enough people in each team, change one bearer after each lap. With very few people, take turns to carry the animal around the space on the towel.

- **Rope-work:** Teach one or two basic knots, such as bowline and figure-of-eight.
- **Build:** Build the set for the story out of Lego® or other construction kit.

Back together

Discuss how the group can be 'faithful' to their friends who are unwell.

Prayer activity

Ask for names of people who need to be healed. Use a different colour pen for each name as it is written in a square on the large sheet of paper to create a quilt effect. When complete, get everyone to hold on to the edge of the paper as the prayers are offered to God.

Challenge

Remember to pray for the person whose name you added to the 'prayer quilt', every day for a week.

Jesus the miracle worker

It is not known why Jesus chose to do miraculous things, but they filled his friends with amazement, awe and fear. Jesus was not just the best human being ever to live. He was also the Son of God.

Key Bible verse

'The things I do by my Father's authority show who I am.'

JOHN 10:25B

Bible links

* Matthew 14:22–33 (Jesus, and Peter, walk on the lake)

You will need
* Bowl or tray of water; blue sheet (or thick paper); towels
* Model boat
* Scouring sponges; chopping board or other protective mat; screwdriver; pieces of paper (6 cm square); hole punch; plastic drinking straws
* Pencils; scissors
* Dark A4 paper; chalks
* Water pistols

Session aim

To know that Jesus did miraculous things.

Gathering activity

Invite someone to stand barefoot in a bowl or tray of water before walking in a straight line across a sheet. Then ask for volunteers to do the same, to see if they can follow the footprints of the first person exactly.

Welcome

Jesus did some astonishing things. Today's story is about something quite amazing. However, it starts with an ordinary boat.

Bible passage

(Show the model boat.) Jesus had been very busy. He had been teaching crowds of people and healing the people who were unwell. He had even fed 5000 men, not even counting all the women and children who'd been fed, too. In the end, Jesus told his disciples to get into the boat and set off for the other side of the lake. He sent the crowds home and then went off on to the mountainside to pray.

The boat (touch boat) had gone some way across the lake. The water was rough because the wind was blowing hard. Suddenly, the disciples saw... well, what did they see? It looked just like Jesus, but how could he be walking across the lake towards them? 'It must be a ghost!' they cried.

'No!' said Jesus. 'It is me, so you don't have to be afraid.'

Peter, the disciple who was always the first to try something even if he hadn't a clue what he was doing, called to Jesus: 'Lord, if it really is you, tell me to come out to you on the water.'

'Why not? said Jesus. 'Come here, Peter.' So Peter got out of the boat (touch boat) and started walking on the water. He got close to Jesus, but then he noticed the wind and the waves and he began to panic. He started to sink into the water.

'Help! Jesus, help me!' he yelled. Jesus stretched out his hand and got hold of him. 'What happened, Peter? You were doing so well until you started to wonder what was going on.'

Jesus and Peter clambered into the boat (touch boat). The rest of the disciples felt overwhelmed by what they had seen. Then they worshipped Jesus.

Ask these questions.

- Why did Jesus not get into the boat with the disciples at the beginning?
- What is the most surprising part of this story?

Response activities

- **Boat:** Place a scouring sponge on a chopping board or mat, scourer side down. Use a screwdriver to make a hole down through the centre of the sponge. Decorate a 6-cm piece of paper to make a sail. Punch holes into the top and bottom of the sail and thread a straw through the holes. Push the straw down into the sponge.
- **Picture:** Use chalks on dark paper to draw the boat on a stormy lake and Jesus walking towards it.
- **Large-scale:** Use water pistols to create a stormy lake.
- **Play:** Repeat the gathering activity.

Back together

Look at some of the boats and pictures that have been made. Discuss being out in a storm. Remind everyone that Jesus has promised always to be with us.

Prayer activity

Sit in a circle and join hands. Pray for everyone in the group together and send a wave right round the circle of hands: the leader raises their right hand, which will raise the left hand of the person holding it. That person then raises their right hand so that the 'wave' is passed right round the circle.

Next, pray for any friends who are absent, and send a wave around the circle.

Pray for people who are scared of something at the moment, and send a wave around.

Finally, pray for all the people around the world who have prayed to Jesus today, that he will answer their prayers as is best for them. Release hands to say and sign, 'Amen'.

Challenge

Sail the scouring sponge boat in a bath or sink, make some waves and remember the amazing miracle of Jesus walking across the top of the lake. People may wish to remember the wave prayers and say them again.

Senses

··

Jesus lived life 'in its fullest' (John 10:10). He used his senses as he met, taught and healed people. He also quoted the prophet Isaiah to highlight the importance of using our senses to understand God. This series encourages everyone to use their own five senses to encounter Jesus.

Jesus said, 'I use stories when I speak to them because when they look, they cannot see, and when they listen, they cannot hear or understand. So God's promise came true, just as the prophet Isaiah had said:

'These people will listen and listen,
but never understand.
They will look and look,
but never see.
All of them have
stubborn minds!
Their ears are stopped up,
and their eyes are covered.
They cannot see or hear
or understand.
If they could,
they would turn to me,
and I would heal them.'

But God has blessed you, because your eyes can see and your ears can hear!'
MATTHEW 13:13–16

A lively song for this series would be 'I'm gonna jump up and down (Be happy)' by Doug Horley.

＊

Touch

Touch is powerful. When used well, touch can encourage, comfort and help. Unfortunately, it can also be used to harm. This session tells of a woman who knew that she would be healed if she could just touch Jesus. It emphasises the positive aspects of touch.

Key Bible verse

Jesus said, 'Touch me and find out for yourselves.'
LUKE 24:39

Bible links

- Mark 5:25–34 (woman who had been bleeding for twelve years)
- John 10:10 (life in all its fullness)

You will need
- Thin card; pencils; scissors
- Several ice-cream boxes, each half-filled with silver sand
- Pipe cleaners
- Construction toy (such as Lego®)

Session aim

To understand that it is possible to know God through touch.

Gathering activity

Play 'Sticky' (see Games, page 249).

Welcome

Invite everyone to imitate (silently) the hand actions of the leader. Ideas include washing hands, cleaning teeth, tying shoelaces, punching, telling off, cradling a baby, searching, pondering, eating with a knife and fork, polishing and drumming.

Repeat the mimes and ask what the movements represent. Talk about the way hands are used—to carry, to hold, to hit, to bless, to comfort, to show, to wash, to help, to hurt and so on. Hands are used in many ways.

Bible passage

Imagine that you are beside a big lake. It is hot and there are lots of people bustling about—and there… yes, right there you can see Jesus getting out of a boat and on to the sandy shore. A big, important man stops Jesus. They talk together, then Jesus walks off with him. There are people pushing and shoving, trying to see Jesus and trying to hear what he is saying. You can see some of his disciples trying to protect him. It is so busy and noisy.

Look! Just over there you can see a woman who really doesn't look very well. You can see that she wants to get near Jesus. And look again! She has stretched out her hand and touched his dusty cloak. At once Jesus spins round, searching. 'Who touched my cloak?' he asks. The disciples laugh. 'Who touched your cloak? There are people all round you, pushing against you, and you want to know who touched you?' But Jesus keeps looking around the crowd, searching.

Then, scared, the woman who had touched his cloak comes over and kneels before him. 'It was me,' she says. 'I thought that if I could just touch your cloak with my hand, then I would be healed. I have been ill for twelve long years and I feel so poorly.'

Jesus smiles down at her and says, 'Your faith has made you well. Go in peace and know you are healed.'

Ask these questions.
- Who used their hands in the story?
- Which is the best part of this story?
- What would you have thought if you had been by the lake that day?

Response activities

- **Hand:** Draw round your own hand on to thin card. Cut out the hand shape and write on it the following words: thumb—HELP; forefinger—SHOW; middle finger—BLESS; ring finger—LOVE; little finger—CARE.
- **Sand:** Use hands to play with the sand.
- **Outline:** Model a hand shape from pipe cleaners.
- **Construction:** Use hands to build something from a construction toy.

Back together

Learn a memory verse: Jesus said, 'Touch me and find out for yourselves' (Luke 24:39). Say each word, pointing to a different digit. (There are ten words if 'your' is split from 'selves'.) Chant it several times.

Prayer activity

Use the hand shapes for five different prayers. Anyone who has not made a hand shape can use their own hand. Start with the thumb and ask for suggestions of who may need God's help. The forefinger reminds us to pray for anyone who points people towards Jesus: again, take suggestions. Next, the middle finger is a reminder to pray for God's blessing. Encourage everyone to name people (either aloud or silently) who need to be blessed by God. The fourth, or 'ring', finger is a prompt to pray for people who love us. Finally, the little finger reminds us to pray for those we care for.

Challenge

Discuss how hands can be used to help, bless, love, care or point others to Jesus in the next few days. Remind everyone that their fingers and thumb will help them remember the five different things.

Look

The Bible encourages everyone to look to the Lord for help (Psalm 105:4, NIV), in the sense of searching to find truth, guidance or aid. There are also stories about the need to use one's eyes, to look closely. Jesus told people when they were sitting on a hillside to look closely at the wild flowers growing around them (Matthew 6:28–30). This session encourages everyone to look closely as they search for God.

Key Bible verse

'Ask, and you will receive. Search, and you will find. Knock, and the door will be opened for you.'
MATTHEW 7:7

Bible links

- 1 Samuel 12:16 (watch the Lord's power)
- Psalm 14:2 (search for the Lord)
- Psalm 34:5 (keep your eyes on the Lord)
- Psalm 141:8 (look to the Lord for safety)
- Proverbs 20:27 (our thoughts search our hearts)
- Matthew 7:7 (search and you will find)
- Luke 15:8–10 (a woman searches for a lost coin)
- 1 Peter 3:12 (the Lord watches over everyone)

You will need
- Ten 10p coins; torch; brush
- A5 thick coloured paper; brown and white paper; foil; scissors; words of Luke 15:8–10 printed out; glue sticks
- A3 paper with grid of squares, prepared as in the 'Shove' activity on page 155; 50p coin

- Kaleidoscopes
- Images of Jesus (see Web references, page 244)
- Piece of string long enough to allow everyone to sit round and hold on to it; a ring
- Chocolate coins

Session aim

To know that it is important to look for Jesus and that he is looking for us, too.

Gathering activity

Search for ten 10p coins hidden around the room. They will be needed as visual aids for today's story that Jesus told.

Welcome

Discuss how everyone got on with last week's challenge of blessing, loving, caring, pointing to Jesus, and helping with their hands. Ask for examples. The last session was about knowing Jesus through touch. Today's is about knowing Jesus through looking.

Bible passage

Have you ever lost something? What did you do? Everyone loses things sometimes. Jesus knew that, so he told this story. (*Place a 10p coin down for each number as it is spoken, to make a row of nine.*) A woman had one, two, three, four, five, six, seven, eight, nine coins. But that was not right—she should have had ten silver coins. They were worth a lot of money. She needed them to feed and clothe herself. There should be ten but now there were only nine.

It was a little dark, so she switched on the light (*switch on a torch and shine it around on the floor*) to help her see. Nothing! She started to sweep the floor *(use the brush)*—still nothing! She looked and looked until suddenly she spotted the missing coin. *(Have the tenth coin in the palm of your hand and 'find' it under one of the children's feet where they are sitting.)* She was so happy that she invited all her friends and neighbours round to have a party.

That is a lovely story, but do you know what Jesus said at the end of it? He said, 'In the same way, God's angels are happy when even one person turns to him.'

Response activities

- **Collage:** Cut out a broom shape from brown paper (cut the ends of the brush to make it frilly) and cut an angel shape from white paper. Make coins out of foil. Stick all these shapes on to a piece of coloured A5 card. Glue the words of Luke 15:8–10 on to the rear of the collage.
- **Shove:** Mark a grid of 8-cm squares on A3 paper. Write each of the following Bible verses on to separate squares, spread around the grid:

  - Just stand here and watch the Lord show his mighty power (1 Samuel 12:16).
  - From heaven the Lord looks down to see if anyone is wise enough to search for him (Psalm 14:2).
  - You are my Lord and God, and I look to you for safety (Psalm 141:8).
  - Our inner thoughts are a lamp from the Lord, and they search our hearts (Proverbs 20:27).
  - Jesus said, 'Search and you will find' (Matthew 7:7).
  - The Lord watches over everyone who obeys him, and he listens to their prayers (1 Peter 3:12).

  Write some actions in some of the other squares (for example, tap your nose three times; jump three times on the spot; wriggle your toes; try to touch your nose with your tongue;

touch your toes three times; scrunch your body into a very small shape).

Take turns to shove a 50p coin across the paper. If it lands on one of the Bible verse squares, talk together about what the verse means. If it lands on an activity square, everyone has to do the action. If the coin lands on a blank square, the coin is passed to the next person for their turn.

- **Kaleidoscope:** Look at the changing patterns in a kaleidoscope and think about the beauty of the world that God created.
- **Pictures:** Look at some images of Jesus from round the world.

Back together

Teach Matthew 7:7 as a memory verse. Use a different hand movement to emphasise each command, as follows: 'Ask' (open hands with palm upwards); 'Search' (shade eyes with hand to look); 'Knock' (mime fist knocking on a door).

Prayer activity

Thread a ring on to a long piece of string and knot the ends of the string securely. Everyone sits in a circle and holds on to the string with both hands. Pass the ring along the string secretly, hidden by the hands. Someone stands in the middle and tries to guess where the ring is. To distract the finder, everyone keeps their hands moving. If the finder guesses correctly, everyone prays for the finder. If they are wrong, everyone prays for the person holding the ring. Keep changing the finder. After several goes, pray for everyone holding the string so that the activity does not become tedious.

Challenge

Give everyone two chocolate coins—one to give to someone else when they tell them the story of the lost coin, and one to eat themselves *after* they have shared the story.

*

Taste

Many children and adults hesitate to taste and try new foods. This session uses the idea of tasting different foods to encourage everyone to try faith in God for themselves, and as a reminder to pray. This might be an occasion to provide noticeably different refreshments from usual to reinforce the theme.

Key Bible verse

O taste and see that the Lord is good.

PSALM 34:8 (NRSV)

Bible links

- Luke 19:1–9 (Jesus calls Zacchaeus out of the tree to have supper with him)
- Luke 22:14–20 (Jesus eats the Last Supper with his disciples)
- Luke 24:13–31 (Jesus is invited to share supper with the Emmaus disciples)
- John 6:1–13 (Jesus feeds 5000 men, plus women and children)
- John 21:1–13 (Jesus cooks breakfast on the beach after the resurrection)

You will need
- At least eight pictures of different types of food; A4 paper
- Paper plates; apple; carrot; prunes (or similar); egg; soft cheese; wipes
- Sticky label with 'O taste and see that the Lord is good (Psalm 34:8)' written on it; thick white paper band (60 x 10 cm); tissue paper (30 x 30 cm); sticky tape; scissors
- Pens; paper
- Children's Bible; music player (optional)

• Chocolate buttons or apple segments; lemon segments; banana slices or dried fruit

Session aim

To understand that it's essential to taste (try out) the things of God to find out if they are true.

Gathering activity

Conduct a 'people-sized' survey of favourite foods. Stick pictures of popular kinds of food on to sheets of paper. Include at least eight foods, each on a separate sheet. Invite everyone to add a tick to all the foods they like, to find out the group's favourite food. When everyone has cast their votes, ask them to stand by their absolute favourite food (of those on offer). Finally, sort the pictures into order of popularity, with everyone standing by their favourite, to create a human bar chart.

Welcome

Review the previous week's challenge of telling someone the story of the lost coin. Whom did they tell and how did it go?

Bible passage

Ask the group to recall any stories in the Bible about Jesus and food. Possible answers include:

• Jesus feeding 5000 men, plus women and children.
• Jesus calling Zacchaeus out of the tree and saying that he would have supper with him.
• Jesus eating the Last Supper with his disciples.

- Jesus being invited to share supper with the disciples he met on the road to Emmaus.
- Jesus cooking breakfast on the beach after the resurrection.

Jesus enjoyed sharing food with other people. Tell the following story.

There is a story, not in the Bible, of a girl who claimed that she would eat anything. If she was offered an apple *(show apple)* she would say, 'I love apple', but then, as she was about to taste it, she would say, 'Yuck!' and refuse to eat any. Her mum would ask her how she knew that she did not like apple when she had never tasted it, but there was no answer to that. When she was offered carrots *(show carrot)*, she would say, 'Yes, please!' but then refuse to taste them.

She kept saying that she would eat anything, but other people started to doubt her. Her aunt would try to tempt her with new things. Her aunt offered her prunes *(show prunes)*. 'Great, prunes!' said the girl. 'Prunes are great.' Then her aunt put them in front of her and suddenly the girl said, 'Prunes are gross.' Her dad gave her a boiled egg *(show egg)* and she was keen to taste it—until the top was taken off. Then she turned up her nose and said, 'Ugh!'

One day, the girl was asked to carry a plate of soft cheese to the table. She had just told her dad that she did not like soft cheese when she tripped. As she stumbled, the plate of soft cheese hit her face *(storyteller puts face into soft cheese)*. 'That's horrid,' she started to say, but she found herself starting to lick her lips as she tried to get the soft cheese off her face. 'That is gorgeous!' she proclaimed. 'I could eat a whole tub of that!'

The Bible says that it is important to 'taste and see that the Lord is good'. Everyone must 'try out' God for themselves to see if what Jesus says is true.

Response activities

- **Chef's hat:** Add the Bible verse sticker to the headband and then decorate around it. Measure headband around head and secure with tape. From the inside push through the square of tissue paper to create a dome and secure with tape.
- **Picture:** Draw your favourite foods.
- **Story:** Listen to the story of Jesus feeding 5000 people, read from a children's Bible.
- **Game:** Play a version of 'Fruit salad' (see Games, page 246). Invite the players to suggest the theme of the game. It could be 'pizza' instead of 'fruit salad', with cheese, tomato, pepperoni and mushroom as the different elements. Another theme could be 'Christmas dinner', with turkey, roast potatoes, bread sauce and Brussels sprouts as the elements.

Back together

Teach Psalm 34:8 as a memory verse. Use British Sign Language to illustrate the verse:

- 'O': use forefinger to point to tip of ring finger on other hand.
- 'Taste': use same forefinger to tap lips twice.
- 'See': use same forefinger to tap cheek below the eye.
- 'Lord': make an 'L' shape with thumb and forefinger in the air.
- 'Good': thumbs up

The song 'O taste and see that the Lord is good' could be played, with everyone singing and signing the repetitive chorus.

Prayer activity

Pass round three different foods in turn and invite people to pray as they taste them.

- Taste something sweet (chocolate buttons or apple segments) and thank God for something lovely that has happened recently.
- Taste something sharp (lemon segments) and pray for something that needs God to sort it out.
- Taste something fruity (banana slices or dried fruit) and thank God for the fruits of creation.

Challenge

Invite everyone, when they taste something sweet this week, to remember to thank God for something good. If tasting something sharp, they should remember to ask God to bless a situation that needs to be sorted out. When eating fruit, they could remember to marvel at the wonders of creation.

＊

Smell

Specific smells can remind us of particular places, people or occasions. The Old Testament has many references to the use of fragrant incense in worship, while Paul wrote to the Philippians that their gifts of money were like 'a sweet-smelling offering... that pleases God' (Philippians 4:18).

Key Bible verse

God also helps us spread the knowledge about Christ everywhere, and this knowledge is like the smell of perfume.

2 CORINTHIANS 2:14A

Bible links

- Matthew 26:6–13 (perfume for Jesus' head)
- John 11:1–44 (the death of Lazarus)
- Philippians 4:18 (sweet-smelling gifts)

You will need
- Range of items that have a distinctive aroma (such as chocolate; herbs; pepper; soap; earth; fresh lemon; lavender; hand cream; wood; perfume or shampoo)
- Barnabas Children's Bible or similar
- Wooden sticks with face shapes or paper plates; pens
- Large cardboard boxes
- Face paints
- Small fabric drawstring gift bags or open-ended sachets made from thin fabric; selection of dried lavender, cloves, cinnamon stick, sprigs of rosemary; fabric glue or tape
- Scented candle
- Spray perfume

Session aim

To understand that the sense of smell can help people to know Jesus.

Gathering activity

Invite everyone to identify different aromas. Either provide different 'sniffing stations', with an item in a bowl covered by tissue, or ask people to close their eyes and sniff different items.

Welcome

Review the previous sessions in the series. Remind the group about knowing Jesus through touch (the woman who reached out to touch Jesus' cloak), through sight (the woman looking for her lost coin), and through taste ('O taste and see that the Lord is good'). Explain that this session is about Jesus and smell, using two very different Bible stories.

Bible passage

Read the story of Lazarus (John 11:1–44) from the Barnabas Children's Bible or another version. Emphasise the phrase 'He will smell very bad' and show a play figure wrapped in a bandage to represent Lazarus emerging from the tomb.

Response activities

- **Face sticks:** Draw a happy face on one side of a wooden stick and a sad one on the reverse (see Web references, page 244).
- **Large-scale:** Set up a box large enough to become a tomb in which a child can hide. Then take turns to be Lazarus emerging when someone else commands 'Lazarus, come out!' Those standing around can pretend to be expecting a bad smell.

- **Face paints:** Draw a smile on to one cheek and a sad face on to the other.
- **Sachets:** Fill a drawstring bag or sachet with herbs and spices. Seal the opening with fabric glue or tape if necessary.

Back together

Ask everyone to close their eyes to imagine the scene as Matthew 26:6–13 is read out slowly. Then point out that pouring perfume over Jesus' head represented a huge outpouring of love and honour for him.

Prayer activity

Light a scented candle and invite everyone to think about how they could honour Jesus, to show how much they love him. Keep a full minute of silence.

Challenge

First, offer to spray people's feet with perfume as a reminder of the woman who loved Jesus so much. Then discuss ways to honour Jesus in the week ahead.

Hear

Hearing is the final sense in this series. Jesus often ended his stories or teaching by saying, 'If you have ears, pay attention!'

Key Bible verse

Jesus said, 'If you have ears, pay attention!'
MATTHEW 11:15

Bible links

- Joshua 3:9 (listen to what the Lord will do)
- Matthew 11:15 (listen well)

You will need
- Pictures/words to illustrate the story: knees, teacher, '10' (x 2), boy, heart, sell, '£' sign (x 3), sad face, camel, needle
- Large heart shapes cut from paper; pens
- Music player; recording of 'I'm gonna clap my hands' by Doug Horley (or similar song)

Session aim

To understand the importance of listening to Jesus.

Gathering activity

Take turns to clap different rhythms that everyone else has to copy. Mix very simple rhythms with more complex ones.

Welcome

Last week's challenge was to find ways to 'honour' Jesus. Was it a difficult challenge? What did anyone do? Explain that this session is about listening. Play a listening game. Go round the group adding words to describe God, in alphabetical order. Listen carefully to make sure to use the next letter in the alphabet (for example, amazing, beautiful, creative and so on).

Bible passage

Place each illustration down to create a timeline as the story is told.

Jesus was walking with his friends when a young man ran up and knelt in front of him (*knees*).

'Teacher!' (*teacher*) he said. 'Teacher, what must I do to get into heaven and live for ever?'

'You know the commandments,' (*10*) replied Jesus. 'Don't hurt anybody or take anything that does not belong to you. Don't tell lies about anyone, and look after your parents.'

'I've have kept all these commandments since I was a boy,' (*boy*) said the young man.

Jesus looked at him with love (*heart*) and said, 'If you have kept all the commandments (*10*), then the next thing you have to do is sell (*sell*) everything that you own and give the money (*£ sign*) to people who really need it. That means you will have riches in heaven and you can come and follow me.'

The young man's face fell (*sad face*) because he was very rich (*£ sign*). He walked away.

Jesus turned to his disciples and pointed out that it was very hard to enter the kingdom of God. 'It is harder for a rich man (*£ sign*) to enter God's kingdom than it is for a camel (*camel*) to go through the eye of a needle (*needle*).

Ask these questions.
- Which part of the story did you like the best?
- What was the most surprising part of this story?

Response activities

- **Hearts:** On one side of a paper heart shape, draw all the things that the rich man in the story might have loved. On the other side, draw all the things that Jesus loves.
- **Retell:** Use the illustrations to retell the story.
- **Stamp:** Take turns to stamp out a rhythm that others have to copy (a repeat of the gathering activity, but using feet).
- **Dance:** Dance along to the song 'I'm gonna clap my hands and stamp my feet', doing the different actions.

Back together

Discuss how it feels if someone does not listen when we talk to them. Share tips for listening well, in class, at home and to God.

Prayer activity

Explain that today's prayer involves listening to what can be heard outside, then inside ourselves and finally from God. Invite everyone to settle down, either lying or sitting on the floor, with eyes shut. First, listen to the sounds around about in the room or outside. (*Allow about 30 seconds for this.*) Then listen to any sounds to be heard inside ourselves. (*Allow another 30 seconds.*) Finally, listen to God. (*Allow at least 30 seconds but extend the silence if concentration is being maintained.*)

Challenge

Ask for suggestions of ways to remember to listen to God in the week ahead.

Prayer

There are many different forms and styles of prayer. It is important to help everyone, of whatever age, to explore the range of ways of communicating and being with God. This will enable them to discover their own preferences and develop a range of approaches to meet particular circumstances. This series looks at some of the various ways to pray and the importance of praying regularly.

A simple song to use for this series would be the Taizé chant 'O Lord, hear my prayer'. The Bible memory verse for this series is 'Pray at all times' (Romans 12:12, GNB). A good way to teach it is to raise one finger on one hand for each word and then one finger at a time on the other hand for the four words of the Bible reference: 'Romans 12 verse 12'.

*

Thank you

Just as children are taught to say 'thank you' from an early age, it is easy to learn to pray by thanking God for all his gifts. By finding opportunities to say 'thank you' to God, we also learn to recognise some of the many gifts and blessings he showers on us.

Key Bible verse

Pray at all times.

ROMANS 12:12 (GNB)

Bible links

- 1 Samuel 1:1—2:11 (Hannah and Samuel)

You will need
- Three long cardboard batons (tubes), one painted red, one brown and one blue
- Plain cloth; plain figures to represent Hannah, Elkanah, Eli and young Samuel
- Cube 'nets' cut from thin card (see Templates, page 236); pens; scissors; glue sticks
- Octons® or other modular construction kit
- Paper
- Bar graph drawn on to paper, with categories of things for which people may wish to thank God: Family; Friends; Food; Fun and Toys; Nature; 'Something Else'; stickers

Session aim

To learn to say 'thank you' to God.

Gathering activity

Hand out three cardboard batons, and explain that the aim is to give them away. If you are given a red baton, pat your head. If you are given a brown baton, turn around. If you are given a blue baton, say, 'Toodle-loo'. (Practise the actions.) Explain that once you have completed the action, you should pass on the baton to someone else as quickly as you can. Make sure to include everyone in the group.

Welcome

Introduce 'prayer' as the theme for the next few sessions. The Bible gives a clear instruction to pray at all times.

Make a fist of both hands. Using one hand, stretch out one finger for each word while saying, 'Pray at all times.' Then, with the other hand, stretch out one finger for each word of 'Romans 12 verse 12'. Then everyone chants the memory verse as they too use their fingers.

Share the idea of remembering to say 'thank you' to God because he gives people so many blessings. A song to sing at this point could be 'Thank you for the world so sweet' or 'Thank you, Lord, for this new day'.

Bible passage

Spread the cloth and introduce Elkanah and his wife Hannah. Explain that Hannah had longed to have a baby for many years. Each year they went to worship at the house of the Lord at Shiloh.

Hannah *(place Hannah figure on cloth, to one side)* went to pray. Eli, the priest *(add Eli figure to other side of cloth)*, was sitting in his chair near the door to the place of worship. Hannah was broken-hearted and cried as she prayed, 'Powerful Lord, I am your servant, but I am so miserable! Please let me have a son. I will give him to you for as long as he lives.'

Hannah prayed silently, but her lips were moving, and Eli thought she was drunk. 'It is time for you to sober up,' he said.

'Sir, I'm not drunk,' Hannah answered. 'I haven't been drinking, but I am so miserable and so upset. I'm praying, telling the Lord about my problems.'

Eli replied, 'Go home now and stop being so sad. I'm sure the God of Israel will answer your prayer.'

'Sir, thank you for your kindness,' Hannah said and she left (*remove Hannah*). She had something to eat and then she felt better.

Elkanah (*place Elkanah figure on cloth*) and his family (*add Hannah*) got up early the next day. They worshipped the Lord and then they went back home. Later the Lord blessed Elkanah (*place hand on Elkanah*) and Hannah (*place hand on Hannah*) with a son (*add Samuel figure*). Hannah named him Samuel because she had asked the Lord for him.

A few years later, Elkanah and his family went to worship at the house of the Lord at Shiloh. Hannah (*move Hannah forward*) and Elkanah (*move Elkanah forward*) took Samuel (*move Samuel forward*). They brought the little boy to Eli (*move all the figures together*).

'Sir,' Hannah said, 'a few years ago I stood here beside you and asked the Lord to give me a child. Here he is—Samuel! The Lord gave me just what I prayed for. Now I am giving him to the Lord, and he will be the Lord's servant for as long as he lives.'

Elkanah worshipped the Lord there at Shiloh, and Hannah prayed a great prayer of thanksgiving: 'You make me strong and happy, Lord. You rescued me. Now I can be glad and laugh at my enemies. No other god is like you. We're safer with you than on a high mountain. Our Lord, you break the bows of warriors, but you give strength to everyone who stumbles. People who once had plenty to eat must now hire themselves out for only a piece of bread. But you give the hungry more than enough to eat. You take away life and you give life. You will judge the whole earth and give power and strength to your chosen king.'

Elkanah and Hannah went back home to Ramah, but the boy Samuel stayed to help Eli serve the Lord *(remove Elkanah and Hannah, leaving Samuel and Eli together)*.

Response activities

- **Thank you cube:** Write or draw something to thank God for on each face of the cube net. Ideas might include food, a person, a place, God, an animal, an event, or 'today'. Glue the cube into shape. If it is tossed like a dice, the face pointing upwards becomes a prompt for a 'thank you' prayer.
- **Large-scale:** Line up at the side of your space. Speak out some suggestions of things to thank God for, one at a time. Invite everyone who wants to thank God for that thing to go to the other side of the space, touch the wall and return. Ideas to get you started include food, toys and friends. Then ask those taking part to come up with ideas.
- **Octons:** Make a structure from Octons, adding one Octon for each thing to thank God for.
- **Alphabet of thanks:** Write a list of 26 things to thank God for, one for each letter of the alphabet. This could be a small group activity.

Back together

Look at some of the 'thank you' cubes and Octon models and encourage their makers to explain what they have made.

Prayer activity

Show the bar graph and explain the different columns. Give everyone two stickers and invite them to place the stickers in the columns naming the things for which they want to thank God. Point out that they can only have two choices, so they may need a little time to make up their minds. When everyone has placed their stickers, let them take a few moments to notice the most popular choices. Then get everyone to bellow, 'THANK YOU, GOD. AMEN.'

Challenge

Point out that a 'thank you' is something given away. Ask for suggestions for a challenge about thanking. Could each person give away five extra 'thank you's each day, or find someone to thank who usually is not thanked?

Please

Some people regard prayer as a kind of slot machine: if they can just make their prayer in the right way, then God will grant their request. It is important to teach that there is no magic or superstitious element to prayer. The Bible instructs everyone to pray for what they need and not to bargain with God for what they want.

Key Bible verse

'Your Father knows what you need before you ask.'
MATTHEW 6:8B

Bible links

- Judges 6:11–40 (God instructs Gideon to defeat the Midianites)

You will need
- Name sheets for Hannah and Gideon
- Sheep's wool (optional)
- A4 card; glue sticks and liquid glue; sequins or confetti shapes; stickers; paper and fabric scraps; pens
- Selection of books of prayers, including those for children
- Noughts and crosses grid drawn on A4 paper; eight squares of yellow paper, four marked with P and four with TQ; eight similar squares of red paper (to fit on the grid)
- Empty, clean milk cartons; camera or mobile phone
- Teaspoons with the letter T, S or P marked on the bowl

Session aim

To know that we should ask God for everything we need, rather than for what we want.

Gathering activity

Organise some 'line-outs' to distinguish between want and need. Ask everyone who wants a new bike to stand at one side of the room, and everyone who needs a new bike to stand at the other side (they remain in the middle if they neither want nor need one). Ask the people who have voted for 'needing' a new bicycle why they think they need one.

Repeat this voting exercise with different items, such as an ice cream, a new mobile phone and God's blessing. During the last line-out, talk informally about what everyone understands God's blessing to be.

Welcome

This session is about Gideon—someone who asked God for something. He asked not just once, but lots of times. He lived more than 3000 years ago. In fact, Gideon lived before Hannah, whose story was told last time.

Display a sheet of paper with 'Gideon' written on it, above a sheet marked 'Hannah', to show a timeline for the two characters.

Bible passage

Practise the refrain 'but God thought he was brave' beforehand so that everyone can join in.

Gideon was a timid man, **but God thought he was brave**.

The people of Israel had not listened to God and they had been conquered by the Midianites, so they were hiding in caves and in the hills. They cried out to God for help and eventually God appeared as an angel to Gideon.

Gideon was a timid man, **but God thought he was brave**.

'Go!' said God. 'Go with all your great strength and rescue the people of Israel from the Midianites!'

'How can I do that? asked Gideon. 'I am weak and not very important.'

You see, Gideon was a timid man, **but God thought he was brave**.

'I will help you,' answered the Lord. 'P-p-please give me some proof that you will help me,' stammered Gideon—for Gideon was a timid man, **but God thought he was brave**.

Gideon cooked some meat and brought it to the angel of the Lord. The angel touched it with a stick and fire came out of the rock and burnt up the meat. Gideon then realised that he had seen the angel of the Lord and he was terrified—because Gideon was a timid man, **but God thought he was brave**.

Gideon still needed more proof that God really wanted him to rescue the people of Israel. So he said to God, 'I am going to put some wool on the ground (*show wool*). If, in the morning, there is dew or dampness on the wool but the ground around it is dry, then I will know that you want me to lead the rescue.'

Gideon was a timid man, **but God thought he was brave**.

And that is what happened. Next morning, Gideon squeezed lots of water out of the wool.

Gideon was a timid man, **but God thought he was brave**.

Gideon was still very anxious. He asked God yet again for the proof he needed. 'This time,' he said, 'can you let the wool be dry and the ground around it be wet? Then I will be completely sure that you want me to rescue the people of Israel.'

Gideon was a timid man, **but God thought he was brave**.

So God did just that. The next day, the wool was dry and the ground was soaked in dew. Eventually Gideon did lead the rescue of the people of Israel, though he kept on asking God for the help he needed.

Gideon was a timid man, **but God thought he was brave**.

Response activities

- **Prayer reminder:** Make a reminder card to 'Pray at all times' and decorate it.
- **Prayer books:** Provide a selection of books of prayers to look at.
- **Noughts and crosses:** Divide players into yellow and red teams and give them eight squares of paper, marked 'P' and 'TQ'. Teams take turns to complete the grid to get three in a row in the usual way, but they must choose whether to say a 'please' prayer (and put down a 'P' square) or a 'thank you' prayer (and put down a 'TQ' square).
- **Large-scale:** Use empty milk cartons to write the words 'Please God'. Take a photo to post on Facebook or text to the group.

Back together

Discuss whether it is easier to ask someone for something or to say 'thank you'. Consider whether it is different when asking or thanking God.

Prayer activity

Ask everyone to choose a teaspoon. Those who have one marked 'T' shake it in the air as everyone thanks God for something. If they have chosen one marked 'P', they shake it in the air as everyone asks God for something. If they have one marked 'S', they shake it in the air as everyone says 'sorry' to God for something.

Challenge

Ask for suggestions for how everyone can remember to ask God in prayer for what they need.

*

Sorry

Learning to say 'sorry' to God, or confessing sin, is a significant step along the path of discipleship. It helps people to get a more accurate view of themselves, accept responsibility for their thoughts and actions, and open themselves to receive God's forgiveness. The response activities for this session do not take very long, as more time will be needed for the prayer activity at the end.

Key Bible verse

Forgive us for doing wrong, as we forgive others.

MATTHEW 6:12

Bible links

- Luke 18:9–14 (the parable of the Pharisee and the tax collector)
- John 4:14 (Jesus provides life-giving water)

You will need
- Sheets of newspaper
- Two teddies; building bricks or mini Jenga® blocks
- Pipe cleaners
- Bubble wrap
- Playing cards
- OHP transparencies or thick clear plastic; washable felt-tip pens; washing-up bowl; washing-up liquid dissolved in water; towel

Session aim

To understand that saying 'sorry' to God helps people to learn to behave as he wants them to.

Gathering activity

Make hats out of newspaper and pretend to be grand (see Web references, page 244).

Welcome

Wearing a special hat can make people feel important or grand. Discuss whether being important or grand makes a person kind or helpful.

Bible passage

This is a Pharisee (*show teddy 1*). He thinks he is a very important person (*put a newspaper hat on to the teddy*). He is a very religious person.

(*Add a brick for each of the following statements.*) He goes to church every week. He prays every morning when he gets up. He always makes his bed—but never anyone else's. He always puts some money into a charity box when he is asked—though he never smiles at the person who is standing out in the street shaking a tin. He has read the whole Bible. He is quick to tell other people that some of the things they do upset God. He makes sure that he never tells a lie. He is careful not to waste time with people who do not go to church. He prays every evening when he goes to bed. (*Push over the tower.*)

This is a man who collects taxes from the Jews to give to the Romans who rule over them (*show teddy 2*). He demands money from ordinary people who don't have very much money. He then takes some of the money for himself. He knows that he cheats people out of their money. He knows that he is not a kind person (*move the bricks around as you talk, not piling them up*).

Jesus told a parable, a special story, to people who were sure that they were good and looked down on everyone else. His story was about two people—one a Pharisee *(touch teddy 1)*, a religious man, and the other a tax collector *(touch teddy 2)*. They both went to the temple to pray.

'The Pharisee stood over by himself and prayed, "God, I thank you that I am not greedy, dishonest, and unfaithful in marriage like other people. And I am really glad that I am not like that tax collector over there. I go without eating for two days a week, and I give you one tenth of all I earn."

'The tax collector stood off at a distance and did not think he was good enough even to look up toward heaven. He was so sorry for what he had done that he pounded his chest and prayed, "God, have pity on me! I am such a sinner."'

Then Jesus said, 'When the two men went home, it was the tax collector and not the Pharisee who was pleasing to God. If you put yourself above others, you will be put down. But if you humble yourself, you will be honoured' (Luke 18:11–14).

Response activities

- **Pipe cleaner 'S':** Twist two pipe cleaners together and form them into an 'S' shape.
- **Large-scale:** Use bodies, lying on the floor, to spell the word 'sorry'.
- **Bubble wrap:** Take a piece of bubble wrap and burst a bubble at a time, saying 'sorry' to God for the different things that are wrong in the world.
- **Building:** Use the bricks to play Jenga or use playing cards to build a house of cards.

Back together

Ask where people might display their pipe cleaner 'S' to remind them to say 'sorry' to God for the things they want to put right.

Prayer activity

Give everyone a strip of OHP transparency (or clear plastic) and a washable pen. Invite them to write or draw something they want to say 'sorry' to God for on to the strip. Explain that Jesus said he is like life-giving water, washing away the sins of the world if people turn to him. Take turns to dip the strips of plastic into the bowl of soapy washing-up water. The plastic will become clean as the pen marks are rinsed off.

When everyone has done this, talk about what has happened to the soapy water (it will have become discoloured) and why. Someone may point out that Jesus has taken on all the sins. Thank God for taking away the sins that were written on the strips and invite everyone to say 'Amen' together.

Challenge

Wear the newspaper hat on the way home and pretend to be important. Then find out what happens if you pour water on to the hat.

*

Praise

It is easy to praise God when life goes well, but it is more of a challenge when we are feeling sad or worried. Matt Redman's song 'Blessed be your name' emphasises the importance of praising God in 'the desert place' as well as in the land that is plentiful. It captures the importance of learning to praise at all times and in all circumstances.

Key Bible verse

You are my God, and I will praise you.
PSALM 43:4

Bible links

* Luke 1:46–55 (Mary's song of praise)

You will need
* Name sheets for Hannah, Gideon, Mary and Jesus
* Parachute (or a flat double bed sheet)
* Heart shape; tea towel; 'holy' sign; handful of sand and paper to sprinkle it on; tiny chair; piece of fruit; 'Israel' sign; rainbow picture
* Building noodles (see Web references, page 245); small pots of water
* Prepared A4 sheets, as described under 'Response activities: Record', page 184; pens; crayons

Session aim

To think about how we can learn to praise God.

Gathering activity

Play with a parachute (or bed sheet) as a group. Then, when it is used for the praise prayers later, everyone will be ready to settle into that activity.

Welcome

Ask who likes being given a sticker at school for doing well. Are adults ever given stickers? Consider whether the person who gives the sticker to someone else enjoys making the award.

Place the Gideon and Hannah name sheets at your side.

Bible passage

This Bible passage is about Mary, the mother of Jesus (*place Mary name sheet below Hannah*). What happened to Mary was almost incredible. She was an ordinary teenager whom God loved. He thought her so special that he decided she was the right person to be the mother of Jesus, God's Son (*place Jesus name sheet below Mary*). God sent an angel called Gabriel, one of his messengers, to tell Mary.

How did she feel when an angel appeared? The Bible says she was confused or troubled, but Mary told the angel that she was God's servant and she was ready to serve him. She set off to visit her cousin, Elizabeth, who was much older than her and was also expecting a baby. Elizabeth said to Mary, 'The Lord has blessed you because you believed that God will keep his promise.' Then Mary burst out into an amazing song of praise to God.

Mary said:

With all my heart (*display heart shape*) I praise the Lord, and I am glad because of God my Saviour.

He cares for me, his humble servant (*display tea towel*).

From now on, all people will say God has blessed me.

God All-Powerful has done great things for me, and his name is holy *(display 'holy' sign)*.

He always shows mercy to everyone who worships him.

The Lord has used his powerful arm to scatter those who are proud *(display paper, sprinkle on the sand and then scatter it with the side of your hand)*.

He drags strong rulers from their thrones *(display tiny chair)* and puts humble people in places of power.

God gives the hungry good things to eat *(display fruit)*, and sends the rich away with nothing.

He helps his servant Israel *(display 'Israel' sign)* and is always merciful to his people.

The Lord made this promise *(display rainbow picture)* to our ancestors, to Abraham and his family for ever!'

LUKE 1:46–55

Ask these questions.
- Which part of the song of praise amazes you?
- Which part of the song do you particularly want to remember?

Response activities

- **Praise sculptures:** Make a sculpture to praise God using building noodles.
- **Listen again:** Re-read Mary's song of praise and discuss as a group why the different objects have been chosen as illustrations.
- **Record:** Divide an A4 sheet into quarters. In large letters, across the top of the whole sheet, write (or type), 'With all my heart I praise the Lord…'. At the base of the first quarter, write 'for he cares for me'; at the base of the second, 'for he has done great things for me'; at the base of the third, 'because he gives the hungry good things to eat', and at the base of the last quarter, 'because he made this promise'. Complete

the prepared sheets by drawing or writing something in each quarter.

- **Play:** Use the parachute to praise God with movement.

Back together

Discuss whether talking about praise makes people feel joyful or sad.

Prayer activity

Gather round the parachute. Think of different things to praise God for and then lift them up in prayer as the parachute is tossed upwards.

Challenge

It is easy to praise God for things that go well. How can we learn to praise God when we are feeling sad or worried? One idea would be to remember to praise God whenever we see a cloud.

*

Praying for others

Learning to pray for other people and recognise that others are praying for us is a further step in spiritual development. Most of us learn to intercede by praying, in the first instance, for our nearest and dearest. It is a sign of growing maturity to start praying for people we have heard about but do not know.

Key Bible verse

First of all, I ask you to pray for everyone. Ask God to help and bless them all, and tell God how thankful you are for each of them.

1 TIMOTHY 2:1

Bible links

• Acts 12:1–17 (Peter is freed from prison)

You will need
- Paper chain links
- Name sheets for Gideon, Hannah, Mary, Jesus and Peter
- A3 poster, headed 'The people of the church are praying'; pens
- Thin card; scissors
- Short lengths of wool or ribbon; a latticed frame (latticed cardboard packaging, stretched out; or string looped in both directions around a shoebox lid; or a simple loom)

Session aim

To understand that God answers prayers on behalf of other people.

Gathering activity

Make paper chains to use during the reading of the Bible passage.

Welcome

Put down the Bible name sheets in timeline order. Ask, or remind everyone, about key parts of these people's stories. Add 'Peter' at the end.

Bible passage

One of Jesus' special friends was Peter. He was a fisherman whom Jesus called to serve alongside him. On the day of Pentecost, when the Holy Spirit came upon all the believers (after Jesus had gone back to be with God), it was Peter who stood up to address the crowds in Jerusalem. Peter went on telling everyone about Jesus, and that made some people very angry.

Explain that everyone is going to act out the story, following the directions of the narrator. Ask for volunteers to play nasty King Herod, Peter, four guards (more if the group is large), an angel of the Lord, and the gate. Everyone else will be the church in Jerusalem, praying for Peter. They have a phrase to repeat: 'The people of the church are praying for Peter' (practise this response).

Nasty King Herod decided to arrest Peter and put him into jail.
The people of the church are praying for Peter.
Two guards tied Peter up with chains (*use paper chain links*) and settled down to sleep, one on either side of him.
The people of the church are praying for Peter.
The two other guards went on duty at the prison gate.
The people of the church are praying for Peter.
Suddenly, when no one was expecting it, an angel of the Lord appeared and there was light inside the dark prison cell (*ask everyone to shade their eyes*).

The people of the church are praying for Peter.

The angel shook Peter by the shoulder to wake him up. Peter got up and the chains fell off. 'Come with me,' the angel said to Peter, and they went past the first guard and the second guard without being noticed.

The people of the church are praying for Peter.

Then the iron gate, which led out into the city, swung open all by itself. Peter found himself walking down the street—and the angel disappeared.

The people of the church are praying for Peter.

Ask these questions.
- What is surprising in this story?
- Who or what is most important in this story?
- Who would you like to be in the story, and why?

Response activities

- **Poster:** Draw a self-portrait on to the headed A3 poster to show all the people who are praying.
- **People-making:** Cut rough outlines of people from thin card, to represent all the people who pray for us. If the bases of the figures are folded back, they can be glued on to a base to create a 'people-scape'.
- **Listen:** Read Acts 12:11–17, as a small group, to discover what happened to Peter after he escaped from prison.
- **Large-scale:** Play 'Fruit salad' (see Games, page 246) as a way of praying for others. Invite the group to name four different groups of people that everyone can pray for (they might be families, friends, people at school, friends at the group). Assign the groups to different places in the meeting space. When the leader calls out, for example, 'Pray for families', everyone has to rush to the place appointed for 'families'. After several turns, choose another four different groups of people to pray for.

Back together

Look at the pictures and models that have been created. Point out people from the group, drawn on the poster, who pray. Then look at the models of all the different people who pray for people in the group. If there is time, talk about what happened next to Peter.

Prayer activity

Invite everyone to choose a short length of wool or ribbon to represent their prayer, and then take turns to weave their ribbon into the lattice to make a pattern of colours and textures. As this will take some time, sing 'O Lord, hear my prayer' together during the activity to help maintain attention. Once everyone has added their prayer, invite everyone to say 'Amen' together.

Challenge

Discuss who are the people that God wants the group to pray for this week. This is a 'secret agent' challenge, because only God will know who is praying and for whom.

*

Listening prayer

Children are often taught to reflect quietly at school, so it may not be difficult to share a time of silent listening to God. This session also underlines that prayer involves two-way communication with God. Everyone needs to learn to move beyond just talking to God and presenting requests, to learning to discern his voice and what he has to say to individuals. After all, Jesus spent much time alone with his Father in prayer.

Key Bible verse

Very early the next morning, Jesus got up and went to a place where he could be alone and pray.

MARK 1:35

Bible links

- 1 Samuel 3 (Samuel learns to listen to God)

You will need
- Analogue radio
- Conch or other large shells (optional)
- Small notebooks
- Stickers saying 'My Listening to God Notebook' (see Equipment, page 251); decorative stickers (hearts, stars, smiley faces, Bible texts and so on)
- Paper; pens

Session aim

To practise listening to God.

Gathering activity

Play a game of 'Simon says' to introduce the theme of listening.

Welcome

What happens if everyone talks at the same time? Try it for a few moments. Now invite everyone to think of something really important that they want to share with the group. Ask if it was possible to hear one person in the general talking. Try again, but with everyone speaking quietly. Ask if that makes it any easier to hear. Ask if whispering all together would help. Finally, pretend to talk, but without any sound.

Christians believe that God is always speaking to people but they often do not stop to listen well. Turn on an analogue radio so that music or talking can be heard. Switch it off briefly and then back on to show that the music or speech can be heard again: the programme has continued being broadcast while the radio was switched off. Then show that the radio may need to be tuned to get a clear signal.

Bible passage

This story is about someone who learned to listen to God. There are actions for the story that need to be practised first:

- Eli: stroke long beard (because he was old)
- Samuel: raise head with a smile (because he was young)
- The Lord: make 'L' shape with forefinger and thumb, up in air
- Sleep/asleep/sleeping: lie down
- Call/called: hands to mouth in a megaphone shape

Samuel served the **Lord** by helping **Eli** the priest, who was by that time almost blind. In those days, the **Lord** hardly ever spoke directly to people, and he did not appear to them in dreams very often. But one night, **Eli** was **asleep** in his room, and **Samuel** was **sleeping** on a mat near the sacred chest in the **Lord's** house. They had not been **asleep** very long when the **Lord called** out **Samuel**'s name.

'Here I am!' **Samuel** answered. Then he ran to **Eli** and said, 'Here I am. What do you want?'

'I didn't **call** you,' **Eli** answered. 'Go back to bed.'

Samuel went back to sleep.

Again the **Lord** called out **Samuel**'s name. **Samuel** got up and went to **Eli**. 'Here I am,' he said. 'What do you want?'

Eli told him, 'Son, I didn't **call** you. Go back to **sleep**.'

The **Lord** had not spoken to **Samuel** before, and **Samuel** did not recognise the voice. When the **Lord called** out his name for the third time, **Samuel** went to **Eli** again and said, 'Here I am. What do you want?'

Eli finally realised that it was the **Lord** who was speaking to **Samuel**. So he said, 'Go back and lie down! If someone speaks to you again, answer, 'I'm listening, **Lord**. What do you want me to do?''

Once again **Samuel** went back and lay down.

The **Lord** then stood beside **Samuel** and **called** out as he had done before, '**Samuel! Samuel!**'

'I'm listening,' **Samuel** answered. 'What do you want me to do?'

The **Lord** said:

'**Samuel**, I am going to do something in Israel that will shock everyone who hears about it! I will punish **Eli** and his family, just as I promised. He knew that his sons refused to respect me, and he let them get away with it, even though I said I would punish his family for ever. I warned **Eli** that sacrifices or offerings could never make things right! His family has done too many disgusting things.'

The next morning, **Samuel** got up and opened the doors to the **Lord**'s house. He was afraid to tell **Eli** what the **Lord** had said, but **Eli** told him, '**Samuel**, my boy, come here!'

'Here I am,' **Samuel** answered.

Eli said, 'What did God say to you? Tell me everything. I pray that God will punish you terribly if you don't tell me every word he said!'

Samuel told **Eli** everything. Then **Eli** said, 'He is the **Lord**, and he will do what's right.'

As **Samuel** grew up, the **Lord** helped him and made everything **Samuel** said come true. From the town of Dan in the north to the town of Beersheba in the south, everyone in the country knew that **Samuel** was truly the **Lord**'s prophet. The **Lord** often appeared to **Samuel** at Shiloh and told him what to say.

1 SAMUEL 3

Response activities

- **Listening activities:** Take turns to clap a rhythm that the others have to repeat. The leader goes first to demonstrate how the game works. Also, use conch shells to listen.
- **Decorate a notebook:** Stick a 'My Listening to God Notebook' sticker on to the cover of a notebook and add other decorative stickers.
- **Sign:** Teach the British Sign Language finger-spelling alphabet (see Web references, page 245).
- **Doodle:** Sketch something from the story of Samuel while listening to God.

Back together

Discuss whether it is easy to listen to God or whether it is something that has to be learned and practised.

Prayer activity

Sing 'Be still and know that I am God' (Psalm 46:10). Repeat so that everyone can join in. Offer the choice of lying down in a space or sitting alone, so that everyone can settle down to listen to God. Explain that after singing 'Be still and know that I am God' once more, everyone will keep silence to listen to God. Allow at least one full minute, or longer if the silence holds and feels comfortable. Ask if anyone feels that they heard God while they were listening.

Challenge

Secret agent challenge: find a quiet place at home to listen to God.

＊

Persistence

It is easy to become discouraged from praying regularly, but Jesus emphasised the importance of being persistent. It is important to encourage everyone to find different ways to maintain interest and different reminders to help them persist.

Key Bible verse

'Ask, and you will receive. Search, and you will find. Knock, and the door will be opened for you.'

MATTHEW 7:7

Bible links

- Luke 11:5–8 (borrowing bread at midnight from a friend)
- Luke 18:1–8 (the widow and the judge)

You will need

- Maze puzzles (with a tiny ball to manipulate around the obstacles, or marble mazes); glitter tubes (filled with glitter and viscous liquid); finger labyrinths (see Web references, page 245); hula hoops
- Small teddy and much larger teddy
- Thick cardboard bases (at least A4 size); drinking straws; sticky tack; large round beads
- Chalk or string
- Plastic or thin wire spirals; beads with holes big enough to fit on to the spirals

Session aim

To know that Jesus told everyone to keep on praying.

Gathering activity

Provide a selection of maze puzzles and glitter tubes for play, as well as some finger labyrinths and hula hoops.

Welcome

Ask if anyone can identify a link between all the gathering activities. They all require persistence if they are to be completed. Jesus told everyone to be persistent, to keep on keeping on, when they pray—not just to pray once and give up.

Bible passage

Jesus told a parable, a special story, about the importance of persistence and not becoming discouraged. It involves a widow (*produce small teddy*) and a big, important judge (*produce large teddy*).

The big, important judge (*touch large teddy*) did not have any regard for God. He did not do the right thing. He looked after himself.

The poor widow (*touch small teddy*) kept coming to the judge to ask for her rights (*move small teddy to tap the large one*). She needed help, but the judge would not listen (*small teddy taps the large one*). The judge sighed (*turn large teddy away*) because the widow kept going on at him (*small teddy taps the large one*).

Eventually, the judge growled, 'I don't have any regard for God or other people, but this woman is getting on my nerves the way she keeps asking for her rights. She will wear me out!' (*Turn large teddy to face small one.*) 'Very well,' he snapped, 'I will make sure you get what is yours by right.' The widow's persistence had paid off ('*walk*' *the small teddy away*).

Response activities

- **Paper labyrinth:** Explore a paper labyrinth with a finger.
- **Bead run:** Make a maze from straws stuck on to a cardboard base with sticky tack, so that a bead will run round it.
- **Bible:** Listen again to the story. If you wish, read on to find out what Jesus said at the end of it.
- **Large-scale:** Use chalk or string to create a large maze to walk through. If you are meeting in a church, use string to tie off the ends of pews (or rows of chairs) to make a giant maze. Check that it is possible to get to the end of the maze.

Back together

Discuss what was most difficult in the different activities. Which of them required persistence?

Prayer activity

Give everyone a plastic or wire spiral and a bead to thread on to it. Invite them to think of something they want to ask God for or about. Then encourage everyone to pray in silence as they gradually move the bead along the spiral. Emphasise that it is not a race; this is a slow prayer activity. For another prayer, ask if they want to move the same bead back in the other direction or if they want to add a second bead of a different colour. At the end, invite everyone to say 'Amen' together.

Challenge

Secret agent challenge: remember to use the prayer bead spiral every day to keep praying.

Fruit of the Spirit

....

Paul writes, 'The Spirit produces love, joy, peace, patience, kindness, goodness, faithfulness, humility and self-control' (Galatians 5:22–23, GNB). These words tell of the qualities gradually developing in maturing Christians who are trying to live their lives for God. They are not a wish list, but qualities that the Holy Spirit can cause to flourish in people as they learn to trust God and become more like Jesus. These 'fruit' can be seen in children just as they may be discerned in adults.

This series of sessions takes each 'fruit of the Spirit' in turn, focusing on what each quality looks like and what it means in terms of behaviour. Each session also highlights a different person in the Bible. It fits well between Christmas and Easter, as the first session looks at the 'un'-love of Herod, but the series could be used at other times of the year. It is a good idea to make a separate A4 card for each of the nine qualities, as they will be mentioned in each of the sessions and used in some of the activities.

A theme song for this series could be 'Peace, perfect peace is the gift of Christ our Lord', inserting the title quality of each session at the beginning of each verse. Love, joy and peace slot in easily, and patience, kindness and goodness will fit if sung as two half-beats. For the qualities with more syllables, adjust the wording to sing 'Faith, faithfulness is the gift of Christ our Lord'; 'Humility, humility's the gift' and 'Self-control, self-control's the gift'. The memory verse for this series is Galatians 5:22-23. See the second session, 'Joy', for a way to learn this verse.

*

Love

This session introduces the theme of the nine fruit of the Spirit. Nearly everyone has some understanding of what love is, so the Bible character featured is Herod, who did not show love.

Key Bible verse

The Spirit produces love, joy, peace, patience, kindness, goodness, faithfulness, humility, and self-control.

GALATIANS 5:22–23 (GNB)

Bible links

- 1 John 4:7–21 (God is love)

You will need
- Heart-shaped sponge or ball, or ball with a heart drawn on it
- Crib set; pictures of an angel and a star; clean clear glass jar
- A4-size paper hearts; pens
- Music player for 'Unto us a boy is born'
- Play dough (include some dark colours)
- Nine cards, each showing the name of one fruit of the Spirit
- Second clean clear glass jar; vinegar; bicarbonate of soda; cloth

---

Session aim

To understand that the Holy Spirit can give love to bless family, friends and the whole world.

Gathering activity

Play 'catch' with a heart-shaped sponge or ball, or a ball with a heart drawn on it.

Welcome

Ask if anyone can remember the good news of the Christmas story. Bring the conversation round to Jesus showing God's love to the world.

Bible passage

The Christmas story was not all good news. Use the figures from a crib set to tell the nativity story briefly, including the pictures of an angel and a star so that the whole story can be seen.

The angels brought good news to Mary, Joseph and the shepherds. What was the good news they brought?

Mary was told, 'You will have a son who will be great and called the Son of the Most High God.'

Joseph was told, 'Take Mary as your wife. She will have a son that you are to name Jesus, because he will save people from their sins.'

The shepherds were told, 'Today your Saviour was born in Bethlehem—Christ the Lord.' The good news was all about God's love for the people of the world.

The magi, the wise people, saw a special star, by which they understood the good news that the king of the Jews had been born.

But somebody didn't think any of that was good news at all. His story is about the opposite of love—hate!

Herod never appears on any Christmas card. He will not be found as one of the figures in a crib set. He does not belong in a story of good news and love. This empty jar (show jar) represents Herod. His heart was not full of love. He was cold, he was calculating and he was cruel. He was king of Judea and he wanted no rivals to his power.

Herod sat in his palace, posing, planning and pretending to be powerful. He heard a disturbance outside in the courtyard—visitors from the east, people who studied the stars—and they were asking, 'Where is the child born to be king of the Jews? We saw his star in the east and have come to worship him.'

Herod was anxious, annoyed and then angry. He was the only king of the Jews. Herod pondered, plotted and pretended to be nice. 'Tell me,' he said to the visitors, 'when you find this baby. I want to worship him too.'

Of course, the wise visitors did find Jesus. They gave him their gifts and they worshipped him—and fortunately an angel warned them not to go back to Herod.

Herod waited, wondered and worried because he heard no more from the visitors. They had tricked him and he became even angrier. Herod was full of rage, wrath and ridiculous fury. 'Kill all the baby boys in Bethlehem!' he roared. You see, Herod's heart was not full of love; he was cold, he was calculating and he was cruel. But an angel warned Joseph to take Mary and little Jesus to safety in Egypt. The good news of God was safe.

Response activities

- **Heart:** Provide pens and a large paper heart shape for each person to decorate with their ideas of the good news that Jesus brings.
- **Stomp:** Explain that everyone is going to create a 'stomp' (avoid the word 'dance') to illustrate each verse of the carol 'Unto us a boy is born!' Listen to the first verse to get a feel for the rhythm. Then discuss a different rhythmic movement for each verse, making sure that the 'Herod' verse is particularly fierce and the last verse is powerful. Then play the carol with everyone performing the different movements in time to the beat.

- **Crib set:** Invite people to use the crib set figures to retell the nativity story. Suggest that they use an empty jar to represent Herod. Discuss whether the clear, empty jar is a good symbol for Herod. Ask what other object could be used to represent Herod.
- **Play dough:** Model something from the passage.

Back together

Introduce Galatians 5:22–23 by reading it slowly: 'The Spirit produces love, joy, peace, patience, kindness, goodness, faithfulness, humility, and self-control.' Then repeat the verses and lay down each 'fruit of the Spirit' card in turn. (This will be explained further in future sessions.)

Explain that God's Holy Spirit can turn ordinary people into something quite amazing. Demonstrate what happens when vinegar is shaken on to a tablespoon of bicarbonate of soda in a clear jar: it fizzes extravagantly.

Prayer activity

Place the decorated heart shapes in the centre of the group and thank God for all his good news. Take suggestions of people or places that need to know God's love at this time.

Challenge

Secret agent challenge: take God's love to someone this week. Do something very kind or helpful without letting the other person know who is doing it.

Joy

What is the difference between 'joy' and 'happiness'? Happiness can come from temporary things, such as eating an ice cream or watching a film. It may involve an element of selfishness: if one football team beats another, their supporters will be happy at the expense of the other team's supporters. Joy, as a God-given gift, has an intensity that blesses other people beyond ourselves and lasts longer. Jesus felt great joy when the 72 trainees he had sent out returned with reports of all they had experienced (Luke 10:17–21).

Key Bible verse

The Spirit produces love, joy, peace, patience, kindness, goodness, faithfulness, humility, and self-control.
GALATIANS 5:22–23 (GNB)

Bible links

- 2 Samuel 6:14 (David dancing)
- Psalm 150:6 (Let everything praise the Lord)
- Luke 10:17–21 (Jesus experiences joy)

You will need
- Nine playground hula hoops (or soft Frisbees or inflatable beach balls); chalk; nine 'fruit of the Spirit' cards
- Modern translation of Psalm 150
- Small paper plates; strips of coloured tissue or crêpe paper; glue sticks
- A3 paper with the words of Psalm 150:6 written in outline on it; pens; crayons
- A4 paper; scraps of brightly coloured paper and fabric; rice or lentils, heart-shaped confetti and so on

Session aim

To understand that God's Spirit brings joy—something deeper than happiness.

Gathering activity

Provide a selection of hula hoops to bowl along or swing around bodies. Substitute soft Frisbees or inflatable beachballs if hula hoops are not available.

Welcome

Challenge everyone to learn Galatians 5:22–23 as a memory verse. Place nine hula hoops on the floor and place one of the nine 'fruit of the Spirit' cards in each hoop. (Draw hoops with chalk if you do not have the real thing.) Ask for a volunteer to jump into each named hoop, in order, as the rest of the group chants the verse. After two volunteers have had a turn, remove two of the 'fruit' cards so that the next volunteer has to remember their positions without the prompts. Then ask for a further volunteer and remove two more of the cards. Finally, ask for someone to jump after all the cards have been removed.

Bible passage

The last session was about nasty King Herod, who was cold, cruel and calculating as he tried to kill Jesus. Today's Bible passage might have been written by King David, who lived 1000 years before Jesus. He was a shepherd, he killed the giant Goliath and he went on to become king of the people of Israel. Through all of this, David was a man of God. He wrote lots of prayers and poems about God that are still used today.

Open the Bible in the middle, to show the book of Psalms in the middle. Read Psalm 150. David also knew how to be joyful—

not just happy, but joyful, knowing that all the help he needed would come from God. The Bible also tells us that David danced before the Lord. The Bible probably tells us more about David than anyone else, apart from Jesus. David was a very special person who really knew God's joy.

Response activities

- **Tambourine:** Make a praise tambourine by decorating a paper plate with joyful colours. Then glue strips of colourful crêpe or tissue paper around the edge to represent ribbons.
- **Decorated Bible verse:** On a sheet of A3 paper, write the outline of the words of Psalm 150:6. Invite everyone to decorate it together, with pens and crayons, as an illustration of joy.
- **Collage:** Create a joyful picture on A4 pieces of paper.
- **Large-scale:** Enjoy playing with the hula hoops, Frisbees or beachballs used in the gathering activity again. *Tip:* this activity will need to be supervised.

Back together

Remind everyone that the session is about joy, and people often sing if they feel joyful. Sing to the tune of 'If you're happy and you know it':

If the Spirit makes you joyful, clap your hands
If the Spirit makes you joyful, clap your hands.
If the Spirit makes you joyful and he leads you to be prayerful,
If the Spirit makes you joyful, clap your hands.

Prayer activity

Invite everyone to think of things to praise God for and, after each suggestion, wave their tambourines (or their hands if they have not made an instrument).

Challenge

Secret agent challenge: look out for someone feeling joyful and then quietly thank God for their joy.

Peace

Peace is much more than the absence of noise or activity. Jesus spoke eloquently of the peace he gives (John 14:27) that would help people not to worry or be afraid. This session focuses on Jesus saying, 'Peace, be still' to the storm.

Key Bible verse

Jesus got up and ordered the wind and the waves to be quiet. The wind stopped, and everything was calm.
MARK 4:39

Bible links

- Mark 4:35–41 (Jesus calms a storm)
- John 14:27 (Jesus talks of peace)

You will need
- Card showing the word 'Peace'
- Blue bed sheet or similar fabric
- A5 coloured paper; stapler; pencils
- Washing-up bowl, one-third full of water; two or three small plastic boats; towel
- Play dough
- Candle; matches

Session aim

To experience something of the peace of God.

Gathering activity

Play 'Sleeping lions' (see Games, page 249).

Welcome

Share the peace by passing a card that says 'Peace' around the group and saying 'The peace of the Lord be with [name]' as each person holds it.

Ask if anyone knows the story book *Peace at Last*. It is a very funny book about Mr Bear, who is tired and goes to bed but cannot get to sleep because the clock is ticking and Mrs Bear is snoring. It is really about being quiet and noisy rather than about the peace of God. When Jesus talks about peace, he means the sense of well-being that can only come from God. Introduce the Bible story by saying that it happened on a very stormy night.

Bible passage

Invite someone to play the part of Jesus and several others to be disciples. In a large group, have twelve disciples, but have fewer in a smaller group, as other children and adults will be needed to play the crowd and to create the storm.

Read the passage below (taken from *The Barnabas Children's Bible*) and use the directions in italics to guide the action. Invite everyone to mime each action, with the exception of Jesus saying 'Be calm' to the waves, which you will prompt 'Jesus' to say.

It was evening, and Jesus was tired after teaching the crowds of people all day.
The crowds press round Jesus, who yawns.

'Let's cross to the other side of the lake,' Jesus said to his friends.
Jesus points across the space.

So they prepared the boat and set sail.
Invite the disciples to sit round in a boat shape.

Jesus went to the stern of the boat and lay down. He was soon fast asleep.

Jesus settles down at the back of the boat shape and goes to sleep.

At first the boat bobbed up and down gently and rhythmically.
The disciples sway gently together. The group who will be creating the storm gather to one side and spread a blue sheet along the floor.

Jesus' friends thought about all they had seen and heard during the day as they made progress across Lake Galilee. But then, as so often happened on that stretch of water, the wind suddenly changed direction. The waves began to crash over the side and the boat lurched dangerously up and down.
The storm group lift the sheet up and down to make rough waves.

The men clung to the mast of the boat. Even the fisherman knew they were in danger. They felt sure they were going to drown, but Jesus was still fast asleep. 'Master, help us!' they shouted, waking him. 'Don't you care if we die?'
The disciples pretend to shout. Jesus wakes up and stretches.

Jesus stood up. He spoke to the wind and to the waves.
Jesus stands up and says, 'Be calm!'

'Be calm!' he said. The wind dropped and the sea was still.
The group with the sheet lower it down.

Then Jesus turned to look at his frightened disciples.
The disciples mime being frightened.

'Why are you afraid?' he asked. 'Don't you trust me?' Jesus' friends were amazed.
The disciples mime amazement.

They had no idea he had so much power. 'Who is he?' they asked one another. 'Even the wind and the waves do what he says!'

Response activities

- **Boat:** Fold a piece of A5 coloured paper in half lengthwise. Make two more folds about 2 cm from the centre fold, one on either side of the centre (to form a W shape). Use a stapler to close the ends of the boat (making sure to include the base so that it is watertight). Flatten the base by pulling the sides apart and pushing down on the centre fold. Write 'Jesus keeps me safe' on the side of the boat.
- **Water:** Play with some boats in a bowl of water.
- **Act:** Retell the story, using the blue sheet to enact the storm.
- **Play dough:** Think about the story, using the play dough as a fiddle toy.

Back together

Look at some of the boats that have been made.

Prayer activity

Light a candle. Explain that you are going to sing 'Be still and know that I am God' twice through and then everyone will keep a minute of silence for peaceful reflection.

Challenge

Either float a paper boat in some water and think about Jesus keeping you safe and peaceful or find somewhere to be peaceful each day as you think about Jesus.

Patience

Modern translations of the Bible often use the word 'endurance' or 'perseverance' rather than 'patience'. While the King James Bible says that 'tribulation worketh patience' (Romans 5:3), the same verse says that 'suffering helps us to endure' in the Contemporary English Version. Patience is a fruit of God's Spirit that grows with his help. Patience is developed by following the promptings of the Holy Spirit.

Key Bible verse

The Spirit produces love, joy, peace, patience, kindness, goodness, faithfulness, humility, and self-control.

GALATIANS 5:22–23 (GNB)

Bible links

• Luke 2:25–38 (Simeon and Anna meet Jesus in the temple)

You will need
- Maze puzzles (with a tiny ball to manipulate around the obstacles, or marble mazes); glitter tubes (filled with glitter and viscous liquid); packs of playing cards (optional)
- Nine cards showing the fruit of the Spirit
- Long cardboard tubes (from inside wrapping paper or kitchen roll); newspaper; sticky tape; cellophane or clear plastic from a carrier bag; rice
- Squared paper; pencils
- Camera
- 'Minute' egg timer that shows sand trickling through

Session aim

To understand that the encouragements of the Holy Spirit teach patience.

Gathering activity

Provide a selection of maze puzzles and glitter tubes to play with. Alternatively, invite people to use the playing cards to play Patience. The adults should be able to help the children get started.

Welcome

To review the Galatians 5:22–23 memory verse, give out the nine 'fruit of the Spirit' cards to nine different people. Invite the rest of the group to sort them into the right order, then point to the fourth card—patience. Ask who thinks they are a patient person. Ask for volunteers to talk about the things that make them feel frustrated and impatient. God wants everyone to learn to be patient through his Holy Spirit, whom he sends to help.

Bible passage

Today's Bible story is about two very patient people who met Jesus when he was still a small baby—Simeon and Anna. They had been waiting to see the Messiah, the Saviour that God had promised to the people of Israel, for years and years and years. They kept coming along to the temple in Jerusalem to pray and wait. They were both very patient.

Read the passage below (taken from *The Barnabas Children's Bible*) as a story. Before starting, invite everyone to point upwards each time they hear the word 'God'.

When Jesus was just over a month old, Mary and Joseph prepared to take him to the temple in Jerusalem. They went to thank God for his safe birth and offer a sacrifice of two pigeons.

As they went into the temple courts, they met a man called Simeon. Simeon had been waiting for the day when God would send his Messiah—the chosen one who would save his people. He believed that God had promised him that he would see this Saviour before he died. When Simeon saw Mary and Joseph and the baby boy in their arms, he knew that the special day had arrived. He took Jesus from them and praised God.

'Lord, you can now let me die in peace, because I have seen with my own eyes the Saviour you have promised your people. This child will reveal your truth to all people on earth and be everything the Jewish nation has been waiting for.'

Mary and Joseph listened with some surprise to his words, but before they had taken it all in, an elderly woman approached them. Anna was a prophetess who had lived in the temple, praying and worshipping God, for most of her long life. She also knew that Jesus was God's chosen one, and she thanked God for him.

Mary and Joseph made their offering. They wondered at all they had learned that day about their baby son.

Response activities

- **Rain stick:** Roll a large sheet of newspaper into a long sausage shape and twist it round to make a spiral. Poke the newspaper spiral down through a long cardboard tube. Put cellophane or plastic over one end of the tube and secure with sticky tape. Add a small handful of rice into the open end and secure this end with cellophane or plastic, too. As the stick is tipped over, the rice will slowly trickle down through the tube, making a sound like falling rain.
- **Maze:** Provide squared paper and pencils to create a maze that wanders from one side of the page to the other.

- **Large-scale:** Working in small groups, use bodies to form the letters of 'PEACE'. (It may be necessary to lie on the floor to do this.) Take photos to print out later.
- **Glitter tubes and mazes:** Play with the tubes and mazes, and reflect patiently.

Back together

Discuss whether any of the activities were easy or a little frustrating. Remind everyone that God's Holy Spirit teaches patience and it has to be practised.

Prayer activity

Ask for prayer requests from the group. When the requests have been voiced, invite everyone to sit silently while watching a timer run through. In a small group, use the rain sticks that have been made during the session. This will create too much disturbance in a large group, so use a minute egg timer instead.

Challenge

A personal challenge: use the rainstick you have made or an egg timer to listen patiently to God.

*

Kindness

Kindness is always welcome when people are unwell or in need of help, but it is a quality that seems to have been somewhat forgotten. However, Jesus displayed kindness when he looked at people with pity, such as when he healed a man with leprosy (Mark 1:40–42).

Key Bible verse

'God's love and kindness will shine upon us like the sun that rises in the sky.'

LUKE 1:78

Bible links

* Acts 9:36–42 (Peter brings Tabitha back to life)

You will need
* Simple jigsaws (20–50 pieces)
* Nine 'fruit of the Spirit' cards; five name cards: Herod, David, Jesus, Simeon and Anna, Tabitha
* Shirt shapes (back and two front halves) cut from sugar paper, with sewing holes (see Templates, page 241); hole punch; wool; blunt darning needles; scissors; pens
* Large nine-space noughts and crosses grid; small cards showing the words help, argue, tidy, moan, look after, ignore, share, damage, encourage, pray, frown, smile; bag; eight sad and eight smiley faces on red paper; eight sad and eight smiley faces on yellow paper (to fit in the grid)
* Long skipping rope
* Paper hand shapes; music player for 'O Lord, hear our prayer' (optional)

Session aim

To understand that God's Spirit helps us to share his kindness.

Gathering activity

Work in small groups to complete simple jigsaws (20–50 pieces).

Welcome

Recently, each session has been about a Bible verse that speaks of the good things God's Holy Spirit produces in people. The fruit of the Spirit is—what? Ask for suggestions and produce the appropriate 'fruit' card as the quality is named. Now invite everyone to put the different good things in order.

Ask if anyone can remember which Bible stories have gone with the first four qualities. Place a name card beside the appropriate 'fruit' card.

- Love: Herod (example of not showing love)
- Joy: David (dancing for God)
- Peace: Jesus (in the boat)
- Patience: Simeon and Anna (waiting in the temple)

Rearrange the name cards to create a timeline—David, Jesus, Herod, Simeon and Anna—and add 'Tabitha', who appears in the book of Acts. She was an early Christian follower who had heard about Jesus from the apostle Peter. She is remembered here because she was kind.

Bible passage

Tabitha, Tabitha loved the Lord.
She made coats and shirts to clothe the poor.
She spent all her time working for God.
With actions, not words, she served the Lord.

Tabitha fell ill and then she died.
They washed her body, laid it aside,
Then sent for Peter to come to their aid,
For Peter knew God's power when he prayed.

The widows were crying, feeling sad.
They showed Peter shirts that she had made.
Peter knelt down alone and he prayed.
He asked for God's power to heal and save.

'Tabitha, Tabitha, get up,' he said
And then he pulled her up from her bed.
He showed them Tabitha quite revived.
The news spread and many, many more believed.

Tabitha, Tabitha loved the Lord.
She made coats and shirts to clothe the poor.
She spent all her time working for God.
With kindly actions she served the Lord.

Response activities

- **Sew:** Using sugar paper patterns for a shirt shape, sew them together with wool. Make holes with a hole punch before the session, to make it easier to thread the wool through the paper. Write 'KIND' on the inside of the shirt so that the word can be seen when the two front sections are opened.

- **Play:** In two teams (red and yellow), play 'happy and sad' noughts and crosses. Take turns to pull out a word from a bag. Decide if doing what the word says would make Jesus happy or sad, and then add a smiley or sad face to the grid. Give a supply of red smiley and sad faces to the red team, and yellow faces to the yellow team. The aim is to get three faces of the same colour (whether sad or smiley) in a row.
- **Skip:** If there is enough space and height, take turns to use a long skipping rope to jump as the Tabitha poem is chanted aloud.
- **Jigsaws:** Play with the puzzles.

Back together

All the activities today involved using hands, so hands are the focus for the prayers.

Prayer activity

Invite each person to write their name on a separate hand shape and place it somewhere around the meeting space. Ask everyone to move round the room, placing their own hand on to each shape and praying for the person named on it to be kind.

Everyone will be moving in different directions at the same time, and some of the children are likely to move quite fast. Play the song 'O Lord, hear my prayer' during the activity (optional).

Challenge

Secret agent challenge: be a kind helper to seven different people during the week, a different person each day.

Goodness

If goodness is the opposite of evil (which can be defined as 'not God'), then goodness conveys a particular sense of the whole glory of God. Many people have lost the positive glow of the word as it has become caught up with codes of behaviour or study: 'Be a good boy!' or 'Good work!' Goodness as a fruit of God's Spirit is much greater than these limited interpretations would suggest.

Key Bible verse

The Spirit produces love, joy, peace, patience, kindness, goodness, faithfulness, humility, and self-control.

GALATIANS 5:22–23 (GNB)

Bible links

- Luke 1:26–38 (Gabriel tells Mary she is to have a baby)
- Luke 1:39–45 (Mary visits Elizabeth)
- Luke 1:46–55 (Mary's song of praise)

You will need
- Angel and Mary figures from a nativity set or similar
- Dark sugar paper; chalks
- Large heart shapes cut from A4 paper; pens; pencils
- Outline of a person on A3 paper

Session aim

To glimpse the amazing fullness of 'goodness' that God's Spirit can bring.

Gathering activity

Ask everyone to move round the group saying something positive to each person—for example, 'You have a lovely smile' or 'I'm glad you are here' or 'God loves *you*.'

Welcome

Ask who the group thinks is the 'good-est', the 'most good', person in the Bible. Who else was full of goodness? Perhaps that honour goes to Mary because God chose her to be the mother of his only Son.

Bible passage

Show figures of Mary and an angel. Talk about Gabriel's visit to Mary, telling her that she was going to give birth to God's Son and call him Jesus. Ask if anyone knows what Mary did next. (She visited her cousin Elizabeth.)

When Elizabeth saw Mary, she said, 'God has blessed you more than any other woman! He has also blessed the child you will have… As soon as I heard your greeting, my baby became happy and moved within me. The Lord has blessed you because you believed that he will keep his promise' (Luke 1:42–45).

When Mary heard what Elizabeth had said, and remembering her puzzling meeting with the angel, she burst out with praise:

'With all my heart I praise the Lord,
and I am glad because of God my Saviour.
He cares for me, his humble servant.
From now on, all people will say God has blessed me.
God All-Powerful has done great things for me,
and his name is holy.

He always shows mercy to everyone who worships him.
The Lord has used his powerful arm
to scatter those who are proud.
He drags strong rulers from their thrones
and puts humble people in places of power.
God gives the hungry good things to eat,
and sends the rich away with nothing.
He helps his servant Israel
and is always merciful to his people.
The Lord made this promise to our ancestors,
to Abraham and his family for ever!' (Luke 1:46–55)

Response activities

- **Praise picture:** Draw a small circle to represent Mary in the centre of a sheet of dark sugar paper and colour it white. Use chalks to create an explosion of colourful praise coming out from the centre.
- **Large-scale:** If you have access to outdoors space, create a similar praise picture as a huge collaborative artwork, using chalk on paving slabs or smooth tarmac. It can be washed away with water after the session or left until the next shower of rain.
- **Heart:** Decorate an A4 paper heart shape with pictures or words to praise God.
- **Body poem:** Work through Mary's song of praise and come up with body movements and hand shapes to illustrate the different statements. For example, place hands over heart for 'With all my heart I praise the Lord'; draw a smile on your face with a finger for 'I am glad because of God my Saviour'; mime a hug for 'He cares for me' and so on. Invite the group to suggest movements phrase by phrase. *Tip:* A leader will need to lead this activity.

Back together

Discuss what a person who shows God's goodness would be like. Answers might include someone who listens to God; someone who prays; someone who does what God requires; someone who shares God's love and so on. Record the suggestions on a large outline of a person on A3 paper.

Prayer activity

Gather round the person outline and pray for the Holy Spirit to fill everyone with God's goodness. Then, using the recorded suggestions, pray for everyone to listen carefully to God, to do what God asks and so on, so that the suggestions become actual prayers for everyone.

Challenge

Secret agent challenge: imagine pointing up to God every time you hear or read the word 'good' in the next week.

Faithfulness

Faithfulness is about persistence, about keeping going when it would be easier to give up, as well as about staying true to God. Contemporary living often values the ephemeral, the instant and the new. God's Spirit wants his followers to develop deep roots (Jeremiah 17:7–8) that can drink from the life-giving water of Jesus (John 4:14). This is done by learning to be faithful.

Key Bible verse

'You may be sure that a servant who is always faithful will be put in charge of everything the master owns.'
MATTHEW 24:47

Bible links

- Daniel 1:1–14; 6:1–28 (Daniel in Babylon and the lions' den)

You will need
- Nine 'fruit of the Spirit' cards; name card for Daniel; toy lions (cuddly or from a zoo set)
- Model or picture of a crown; model or picture of an angel
- 8-cm rings of thin card, with a 2-cm hole cut out of the centre (two rings per person); lengths of wool; sharp scissors
- Storybook version of Daniel and the lions

Session aim

To know that God's Spirit helps people to learn to be faithful.

Gathering activity

Play 'God commands'. Ask people to stand up if they think this is
what God commands and sit down if they think God doesn't want
them to do it: pray every day; scowl; read the Bible; break a friend's
toy; be still and listen to him; waste food; tell others about Jesus;
steal something; look after lonely people; get in a rage; be kind.

Welcome

Today's Bible passage is about someone who was not a secret agent.
He was very brave and faithful to God (*show 'Faithfulness' card*) and
his name was Daniel (*show 'Daniel' card*). He had a close meeting
with some lions (*show the toy lions*).

Bible passage

Demonstrate the letter 'F' in British Sign Language so that everyone
can sign 'F' every time the word 'faithful' is mentioned. (Tap the
first two fingers of one hand on top of the first two fingers of the
other hand.)

This is the story of Daniel, a faithful man. Daniel always remembered
to pray to God. Daniel was a prisoner in Babylon but he remained
faithful to God.

Nebuchadnezzar was the king of Babylon (*show the crown*) and
he decided to use Daniel in his royal court. Because Daniel was
faithful to God, Daniel decided not to eat the food or drink the
wine provided for the court; he would eat just vegetables and
drink plain water. He also remembered to pray. Daniel had a lot of
adventures in the court of King Nebuchadnezzar but he still stayed
faithful to God.

Then came a new king, Darius. Daniel was good at his job but
the other officials in the court did not like him. They started trying

to spot Daniel doing something wrong, but Daniel was a faithful man—faithful to God first, then faithful to the king he worked for.

The other officials came up with a nasty plan. They asked King Darius to give an order that no one should make any request of a god or of any man other than King Darius himself. When Daniel heard about this, he knew what he had to do. He would not give up praying to God, so he went home and did just that. Daniel prayed to God. He prayed to God three times a day, kneeling by his window so that everyone could see what he was doing. Daniel was a faithful man.

Of course, the nasty officials told the king that Daniel was acting against his order. King Darius was upset but he had to stand by what he had decreed. The king ordered Daniel to be thrown into the den of lions (*show the toy lions*). Daniel was left there all night and the king was worried.

Early next morning, the king rushed to the lions' den and called out, 'Daniel, are you there?' The king listened anxiously. Then, from the depth of the den, Daniel called back, 'Your majesty! God sent his angel (*show the angel*) to shut the mouths of the lions. I have been kept quite safe.'

King Darius was delighted and had Daniel released. He wrote to all his people to tell them to respect Daniel's God. All this happened because Daniel was a faithful man.

Response activities

- **Pompoms:** Give each person two cardboard rings. Lay the rings one on top of the other and wrap wool around them until no more wool will fit through the centre hole. Use sharp scissors to cut through the wool, right round the outside of the ring. Gently pull the card rings apart slightly and tie a length of wool tightly around the centre, between the rings. Pull the card rings off completely and fluff up the wool to make a ball. This activity takes a long time of 'faithful' activity, so may need to be completed at home. See the Web references (page 245) for more detailed instructions.

- **Listen again:** Read aloud the story of Daniel from a storybook.
- **Stomp:** Learn the words of this very old chorus and stomp around to the beat as the words are chanted. Swing your arms as well (think of the walk done by the rock group Madness).

    'Dare to be a Daniel,
    Dare to stand alone!
    Dare to have a purpose firm!
    Dare to make it known.'
- **Retell:** Use the toy lions and the angel and crown models or pictures to retell Daniel's story.

Back together

Talk about people in the group who are faithful—for example, the person who faithfully provides refreshments each time or sets out the room. Take the opportunity to thank them.

Prayer activity

Daniel was faithful in prayer. Pass a toy lion around the group and ask each person to say, if they wish, if there is anything they need God to help them with in the next few days. Once the lion has been passed to everyone, invite them all to say 'Amen'. Then pass round the angel model or picture and pray for God's protection for each person in turn and by name. Again, conclude by saying 'Amen' together.

Challenge

Remember to be faithful to God in prayer this week. Ask if anyone can suggest a good way to remember to pray at least once each day. Discuss whether this should be a 'secret agent' challenge.

*

Humility

Sometimes translated as 'gentleness', humility means having an accurate understanding of ourselves—neither being puffed up with pride nor viewing ourselves as less than we are. The only one who should weigh people up is God. The word 'humility' comes from the Latin word *humus*, meaning 'earth', so it could be said that people who show humility have their feet on the ground. This session encourages everyone to have a clear, well-balanced view of themselves with the help of the Holy Spirit.

Key Bible verse

Clothe yourselves with humility.

1 PETER 5:5 (NIV)

Bible links

- Luke 9:46–48 (who is the greatest?)
- Luke 14:8–11 (how to behave at a wedding)

> **You will need**
> - Thin card cut to A6 size; foil oblongs, 1 cm larger all round than the A6 card; glue sticks; stickers saying 'Clothe yourselves with humility (1 Peter 5:5)'; happy and unhappy face stickers
> - Paper; pens
> - Playmobil® or similar people figures
> - Cross or star shape

Session aim

To understand that God's Spirit teaches people to see themselves as they really are—with humility.

Gathering activity

Ask everyone to stretch up, crouch down or just stand normally, according to whether they think they fit the description you give. For example, 'Stretch up tall if you are *good at sums*; crouch down small if you are not; or just stand still if you think you are somewhere in the middle.'

Substitute each of the following descriptions in turn: 'Stretch up tall if you are a good singer... a strong swimmer... kind... noisy... full of energy... able to play a musical instrument... always helpful... generous... patient... cheerful... tidy... if you pray every day'.

Welcome

Ask if anyone can remember the Bible verse from Galatians about the fruit of the Spirit. Repeat it together a couple of times. Discuss the idea of humility. It means having an accurate understanding of ourselves—so people should not boast that they are good at something if they are not, but nor should they pretend they're not good at something if they are.

Often we get feedback about how we are from other people. Sometimes the feedback is helpful and sometimes other people get it wrong. The only one who really sees people as they are is God.

Bible passage

Ask who has ever had an argument at home, school or work about who is the best at something or the most important. Some of Jesus' friends, the disciples, did just that. Read Luke 9:46–48. Jesus' teaching, that the least among us is the greatest, sounds upside-down.

Jesus also told a story about people being invited to a wedding. He said that if you get there early, you shouldn't grab the best place. Someone more important than you might come along later, and then you will be turned out of your seat. That would be embarrassing. He said again that anyone who puffs themselves up with importance will be put down, while anyone who behaves with humility might be promoted or raised higher.

Response activities

- **Mirror:** A mirror helps people to see themselves as they really are and reminds them to be humble (self-aware). Lay an A6 card on to the less shiny side of a foil oblong, leaving a border of foil showing all round. Fold in the foil and glue it down on to the back of the card. Turn the card over so that you can see the mirrored side, and add a sticker saying 'Clothe yourselves with humility (1 Peter 5:5)' in a bottom corner. Finally, add a happy and an unhappy face sticker, one in each of the top corners.
- **Move:** Play a version of 'Duck, duck, goose' (see Games, page 246) using the words 'Servant, servant, guest'.
- **Design:** Imagine that Jesus was coming to your gathering, and design a seating plan. Where would Jesus sit? Where would you sit? Where would you place the group leader and your friends?
- **Play:** Use play figures to retell the story.

Back together

Talk about some of the different gifts and talents that people in the group have. Be sure to include the adults in this discussion.

Prayer activity

Work round the group, thanking God for a particular quality or talent of each person. Pass a special cross or star shape to each person in turn as they are prayed for. You might say, 'Thank you, God, for [name] and his lovely smile/the lovely cakes he makes/her willingness to tidy up.'

Challenge

Secret agent challenge: every time you see a mirror or look at the one you made today, ask God to show you something you are good at or help you practise something that you are not so good at.

*

Self-control

Jesus, by the power of the Holy Spirit, showed immense self-control throughout his life, but particularly from the time he went into Jerusalem until he died. The Holy Spirit can teach everyone to exercise more self-control as they grow in discipleship.

Key Bible verse

The Spirit produces love, joy, peace, patience, kindness, goodness, faithfulness, humility, and self-control.
GALATIANS 5:22–23 (GNB)

Bible links

• Mark 14:32—15:37 (from Gethsemane to the crucifixion)

You will need
• Dark paper or cloth; moss; picture of praying hands; sword; purple ribbon; cross
• Wooden crosses (see Web references, page 245); pens; pencils
• Simple storybooks telling the Easter story
• Paper; chalks
• Candle; matches

Session aim

To understand how much self-control Jesus showed in the last days of his life.

Gathering activity

Stand on one leg for one minute. Now repeat, but this time you must not speak, smile or wobble.

Welcome

Review the 'fruit of the Spirit' memory verse by using hand movements: love (make heart shape with thumbs together and fingers folding inwards); joy (wave), peace (rock a baby), patience (rest head on hand), kindness (hold out hand), goodness (thumbs up), faithfulness (draw spiral with finger), humility (make square shape to represent a mirror), self-control (point to self).

Bible passage

In the days leading up to Easter, it is time to think about Jesus going to die *(lay down the dark paper or cloth)*. He had gone to Jerusalem with his friends and they had shared a special meal. Afterwards he took his disciples to the Garden of Gethsemane *(place moss on paper or cloth)*. He asked them to keep watch with him while he prayed *(show praying hands picture)*, but they fell asleep.

Jesus was sad that his friends slept when he had asked them to support him, but he did not get angry.

After a while, soldiers came to arrest him, and one of his own friends, Judas, pointed him out. There was an angry scene and another of Jesus' friends drew his sword *(place sword on paper or cloth)* and wounded one of the enemy. Again, Jesus was sad and told his friend to put away his sword. He did not get angry.

Jesus asked the men who had come to arrest him why they had brought weapons when they could have taken him away as he sat teaching in the temple. The disciples ran away, so Jesus was left on his own.

Jesus was taken to the high priest. His enemies taunted him

and spat on him, but Jesus kept his self-control. They took Jesus to Pontius Pilate, the Roman governor, who questioned him, and Jesus kept his self-control.

The soldiers mocked Jesus. They put a purple robe *(place purple ribbon on paper or cloth)* and a painful crown of thorns on him. They jeered and hit and spat, and Jesus kept his self-control because God's Holy Spirit was giving him strength.

They made Jesus carry his own cross, and Jesus kept his self-control. Jesus died on the cross *(place cross on paper or cloth)*.

Response activities

- **Cross:** Use pens or pencils to decorate a wooden cross.
- **Holy Week:** Read a different account of Holy Week and Easter.
- **Retell the story:** Using the different objects displayed on the paper or cloth, tell the story again.
- **Large-scale:** Use chalks to draw and decorate a large cross on paper.

Back together

It was a dark day, a Friday, when Jesus was killed, but that was not the end of the story. God's love for the world, for us, was much greater than death. On the following Sunday, when some of the women who followed Jesus went to the tomb where he had been buried, they did not find his body. Instead, there was an angel *(light a candle)* who told them that Jesus had been raised to new life.

Prayer activity

Sit and watch the candle as you reflect that Jesus, the light of the world, died for everyone in the group, so that they can live with him for ever if they choose.

Challenge

On Easter Day (or on Sunday) remember how much Jesus loves (*point at individuals*) you, and you, and you: all of you! Everyone is invited to be part of God's amazing family.

✱

Templates

Invitation postcard example

Cube net

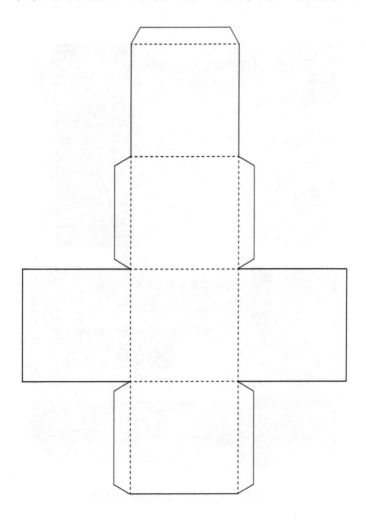

Star

Go to www.barnabasinchurches.org.uk/9781841016627 to download and print at A4 size

Game

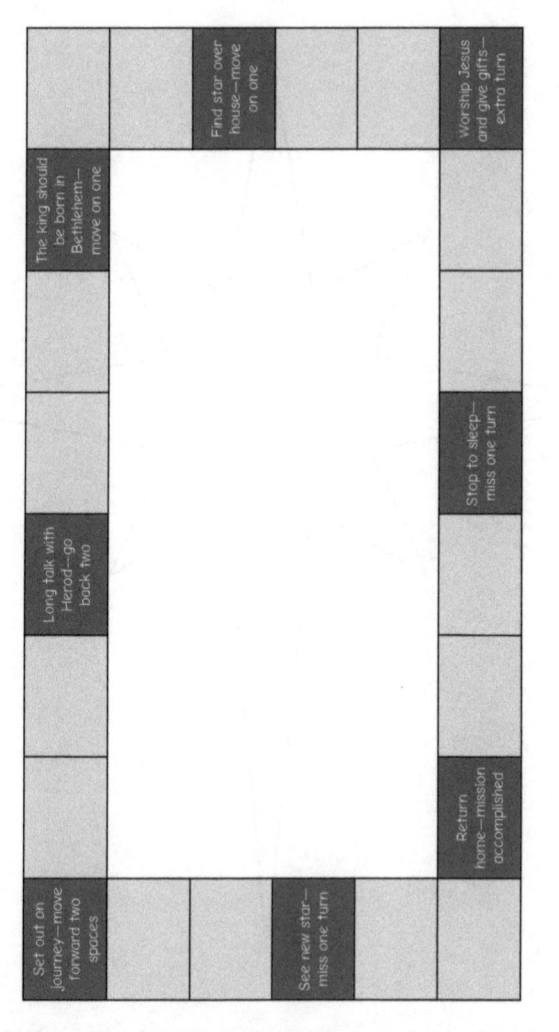

Go to www.barnabasinchurches.org.uk/9781841016627 to download and print at A4 size

Ecclesiastes 3:1 colouring outline

Reproduced with permission from *50 Praise, Pray and Play Sessions* by Rona Orme (Barnabas for Children, 2015) www.barnabasinchurches.org.uk

Go to www.barnabasinchurches.org.uk/9781841016627 to download and print at A4 size

Holy Week and Easter cube net

Go to www.barnabasinchurches.org.uk/9781841016627 to download and print at A4 size

Shirt shape

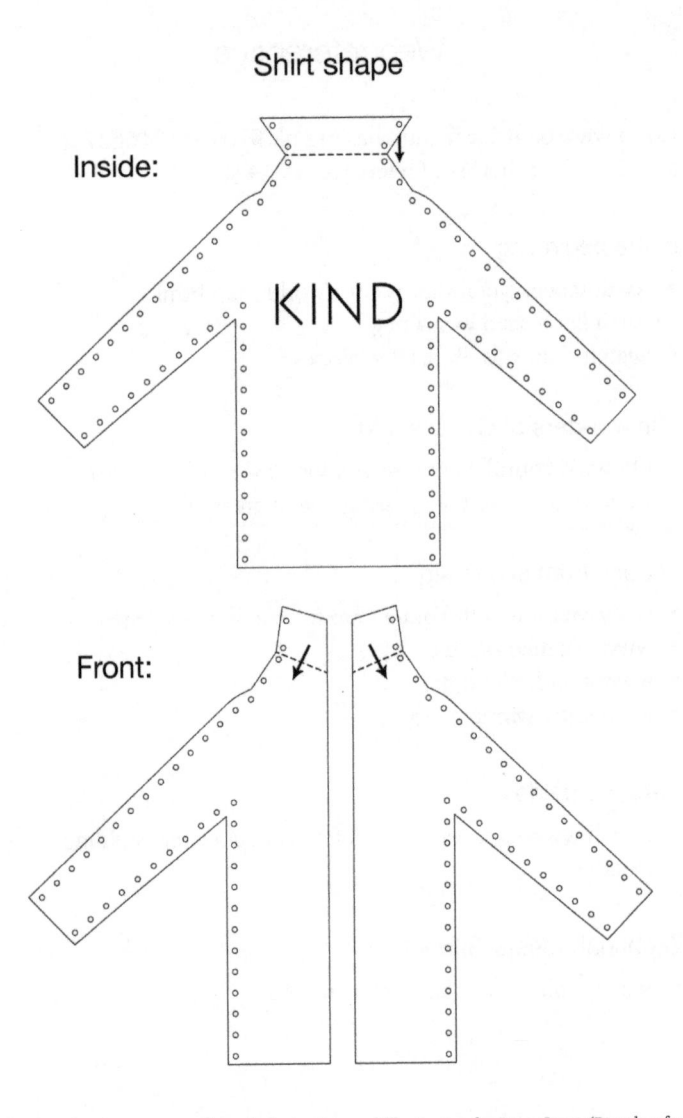

Inside:

KIND

Front:

Reproduced with permission from *50 Praise, Pray and Play Sessions* by Rona Orme (Barnabas for Children, 2015) www.barnabasinchurches.org.uk

Go to www.barnabasinchurches.org.uk/9781841016627 to download and print at A4 size

Web references

Go to www.barnabasinchurches.org.uk/9781841016627 to download and print this list of references at A4 size.

In the beginning
- www.wipeeasytablecloths.com/world-map.html (for a floor-sized world map).
- Search online for 'inflatable globes'.

The wonders of God's world
- On www.youtube.com, search for 'Powers of Ten (1977)', a video that shows the amazing size of creation.

Water—from sea to sip
- www.wikihow.com/Fold-a-Cup-from-a-Sheet-of-Paper
- www.wateraid.org/uk
- www.worldtoilet.org
- www.toilettwinning.org

Nature provides
- Search www.ss-services.co.uk for Biodegradable Building Noodles.

Zechariah meets Gabriel
- Search online for 'blank scraperboard'.

Mary meets Gabriel

- On www.youtube.com, search for 'Bible Animation 1 Gabriel Visits Mary'.

Wise people meet Jesus

- On www.youtube.com, search for 'A Wriggly Nativity Christmas animation for kids'.

Ash Wednesday/The armour of God/Towards Easter/Ascension

- www.going4growth.org.uk/downloads/Church_Year_diagram. pdf

Towards Easter

- Search online for 'plastic Easter egg shells'.

Easter morning

- On www.youtube.com, search for 'Animated The Easter Story. mp4'

Surprised by Jesus

- On www.youtube.com, search for 'On the road to Emmaus cibolo creek video'.

Breakfast on the beach

- http://hellejorgensen.typepad.com/gooseflesh/2007/02/plastic_ bag_yar.html (to make plastic strips from carrier bags, use the first five pictures)

Pentecost

- Search online for 'Candle decorating pens'.

Jesus the teacher (1)

- www.trusselltrust.org (food banks)
- www.wateraid.org (clean water project)
- www.freecakesforkids.org.uk (birthday cakes for children who would not get one otherwise)

Jesus the teacher (2)

- www.enchantedlearning.com/crafts/Paperhouse.shtml

Jesus the friend (1)

- www.youtube.com, search for 'The Man Lowered Through the Roof Kids Hub TV'.

Jesus the friend (2)

- Search online for 'lolly or wooden craft sticks'.

Jesus the healer

- www.animatedknots.com

Look

- www.jesusmafa.com/?lang=en (images of Jesus from Africa) or search online for images of Jesus.

Smell

- www.ss-services.co.uk/craft-supplies/wood/craft-sticks-faces-set-of-36
- Search online for 'drawstring gift bags'.

Sorry

- www.wikihow.com/Make-a-Paper-Hat (use first six instructions)

Praise

- On www.youtube.com, search for 'Matt Redman and the London Community Gospel Choir Blessed Be Your Name'
- Search www.ss-services.co.uk for Biodegradable Building Noodles.

Listening prayer

- http://homepage.ntlworld.com/ian.barnsley/bslsite/z.html (finger-spelling alphabet for British Sign Language)

Persistence

- http://labyrinthsociety.org/download-a-labyrinth

Love

- On www.youtube.com, search for 'Love Monkey Edward Monkton'.

Joy

- On www.youtube.com, search for 'The Pig of Happiness Edward Monkton'.

Faithfulness

- www.wikihow.com/Make-a-Pom-Pom
- http://homepage.ntlworld.com/ian.barnsley/bslsite/z.html (finger-spelling alphabet for British Sign Language)

Self-control

- www.wooden-crosses.co.uk/wooden-cross-activity.htm

All web links are correct at time of going to press.

Reproduced with permission from *50 Praise, Pray and Play Sessions* by Rona Orme (Barnabas for Children, 2015) www.barnabasinchurches.org.uk

Games

Duck, duck, goose

Players sit in a circle facing inwards. The person who is 'It' walks round the outside of the circle, gently tapping each player's head in turn and saying 'duck'. When they say 'goose' instead of 'duck', the player they have tapped has to stand up and chase them round the circle. If the person who is 'It' reaches the empty space without being tagged, they sit down and the 'goose' becomes 'It'. If not, they continue to be 'It' for another turn.

Fruit salad

Choose four different items to represent the main elements of the story—for example, apple, orange, pear and banana. Ask everyone to sit in a circle, and then move round the group, naming each person in turn as one of the chosen items. When that item is called out—for example, 'apple'—people who have been named 'apple' have to change places with each other. Name the different items in turn and, from time to time, call out a name that applies to the whole group—in this instance, 'fruit salad'. Everyone then has to get up and change places.

Grandma's shopping game

The first person says, 'I went shopping and I bought a DVD.' The second person says, 'I went shopping and I bought a DVD and two bananas.' The third person repeats, 'I went shopping and I bought a DVD, two bananas and…', adding their own idea. Keep going until the list becomes too long to remember.

Hoop promise

Five or more people join hands in a ring, with one pair joining hands *through* a hula hoop. Everyone says, 'I promise not to let go hands until the hoop has passed right round the circle.' Then gradually pass the hoop round the circle by stepping through it.

Hopscotch

Draw a hopscotch grid (1–10) on the floor, pairing the squares numbered 3 and 4, and 7 and 8. Each person has a stone to throw. They must first throw it on to square 1, which they hop over before hopping up to the end of the grid and back, pausing to pick up their stone. On their next turn, they throw the stone on to square 2 and repeat the process. If they miss the square they are aiming for with their throw, they miss their turn. If they put more than one foot in each square, they must also miss their next turn.

Hot potato

Players stand or sit in a circle and pass a potato round as the music plays. When the music stops, whoever is holding the 'hot' potato has to drop out.

Human spelling

Everyone uses the initial letter of their first name to help spell out words. For example, Jasmine, Oliver, Hatty and Noah could come together to spell the name 'John'.

Human dominoes

As an example, the first person says that their favourite colour is blue (waving their left hand) and they like giraffes (waving their right hand). Another person whose favourite colour is blue holds the left hand of the first person, and says that they are good at maths. Now another person is needed—either one who likes giraffes (and holds the right hand of the first person) or one who is good at maths (and holds the left hand of the second person, naming a new category for joining the chain). The aim is to get everyone joined on to the chain.

Line-out

Everyone who agrees strongly with a statement stands at one end of a line, while everyone who disagrees strongly stands at the other end. People who are not sure stand somewhere along the line to indicate their views.

Memory game

Beforehand, place several items on a tray and cover it with a cloth. Produce the covered tray and explain that everyone will have 30 seconds to memorise everything that is on the tray. Uncover the tray for half a minute, then cover it and remove it from sight for another 30 seconds. Invite people to take turns to name all the items they can remember. Note down the answers. Finally, uncover the tray once more and see how well the items have been remembered.

Musical chairs

Set out enough chairs (or sheets of newspaper) for everyone in the group, and then take one away. When the music plays, everyone walks around. When the music stops, everyone has to sit on a chair. The person left without a chair is out. Remove another chair for each round. The winner is the person sitting on the final chair.

Port and starboard

Each corner of the space represents one key word in the theme you are illustrating, while the centre of the space represents a summary word or overall theme. When the leader calls out a word, everyone has to run in that direction. It is a good way to introduce or teach the key words of a Bible story.

Simon says

The leader calls out actions that everyone has to perform, but moves should only be made if the leader first says 'Simon says' or another phrase of command. The most obvious alternative command phrase could be 'Jesus says'. If the command phrase is omitted, no one should make a move or they are 'out'.

Sleeping lions

Everyone lies on the floor and pretends to be asleep. Anyone who is seen to move or heard to make a noise is 'out'.

Sticky

Everyone moves around the space. The person who is 'sticky' tags someone so that they become a 'sticky' pair. This pair now tries to tag a third person to become a three-person 'sticky'. The aim is to get everyone stuck together. A different way of playing this game is to appoint someone else to be 'unstuck'. They try to touch the most recent person to be stuck to 'sticky' and release them.

Who's welcome?

Say, 'You are welcome to come into the centre if…', then add a category, such as '… you are wearing red socks' or '… you had cornflakes for breakfast' or '… you have ridden on a bus this week' or '… you have a pet' or '…you have cleaned your teeth today' and so on. Vary the categories, but use the least likely first, so that only a few people come forward. Make sure the last category named will guarantee that everyone is included.

Equipment

A number of items will be needed again and again, so it is helpful to build up some basic kit. However, it is not necessary to provide enough pairs of scissors (for example) to allow everyone to use a pair at the same time. Waiting a short time to use resources can help to teach the value of sharing.

Basic equipment will include the following:

- A4 paper and thin card in a choice of colours
- Plain paper plates
- Felt-tip pens, pencils, coloured chalks and pastel crayons
- Scissors for children and adults
- Box of scraps for collage, including various kinds of paper, fabric, ribbon and so on
- Glue sticks
- 'Neutral' people figures for storytelling. Wooden Godly Play figures (available from www.godlyplay.org.uk/materials/suppliers) work well. Otherwise, use everyday Playmobil® figures
- Water pistols if you have access to outside space. Another way of doing large-scale and wet activities is to use large house-painting brushes and tubs of plain water
- World map, preferably floor-size with a plastic surface so that stickers can be put on to it
- 'Peace' sign
- Pipe cleaners
- Large cardboard boxes—those that contain either five packs of A4 paper or six bottles of wine. These are suitable for construction and large-scale activities. Bigger boxes would be even more fun but may require too much storage space.
- Play dough (home-made or bought)

- Sand (silver, from a garden centre)
- Clean shallow food trays that can be half-filled with sand
- First aid kit

Make your own scraperboard

Use thick paper, such as sugar paper, or thin card. Cover with wax crayon—either a single colour or a rainbow of colours—pressing down hard. Then paint over the entire surface with ready-mixed paint. Black is the traditional colour for the surface of scraperboards but any dark colour could be used.

Stickers

A number of craft activities involve the use of stickers with Bible verses pre-printed on them. These can be prepared on a home computer with a label printer. However, verses can also be printed multiple times on a plain sheet of paper, cut up and glued on.

Resources

Songs

A leader can introduce these songs unaccompanied. With better facilities, or a stronger music tradition, you can build up a simple repertoire. In an all-age group, avoid songs written specifically for children. Men and older boys do not necessarily enjoy imagining themselves to be butterflies.

- All good gifts around us (the chorus of 'We plough the fields and scatter')
- Be still and know that I am God (HON 52)
- Blessed be your name (Matt Redman)
- Born in the night, Mary's child (HON 65)
- Father, we adore you (HON 125)
- Gloria, gloria (HON 157)
- Glory to God, glory to God (HON 161)
- He is Lord, he is Lord (HON 204)
- I'm gonna jump and down (Doug Horley)
- He's got the whole world in his hands (HON 206)
- Jesus, remember me (HON 276)
- Jesus, you're my superhero (Hillsong)
- My God is so big, so strong and so mighty
- O come let us adore him (chorus of 'O come, all ye faithful)
- O Lord, hear my prayer (HON 379)
- O taste and see that the Lord is good
- Peace, perfect peace (HON 414)
- Thank you for the world so sweet
- Thank you, Lord, for this new day (HON 468)
- Unto us a boy is born (HON 526)
- Wait for the Lord (Taizé) (HON 528)
- We are marching in the light of God
- We have a king who rides a donkey

HON = Hymns Old and New

Publicity

- Vistaprint (for postcards)
- Websites such as www.wherecanwego.com

Websites

- http://homepage.ntlworld.com/ian.barnsley/bslsite/bslindex.html (alphabet in British Sign Language)
- www.ss-services.co.uk for resources such as pipe cleaners, wooden people sticks and so on
- www.throughtheroof.org

Index of key Bible verses

Index of Bible links